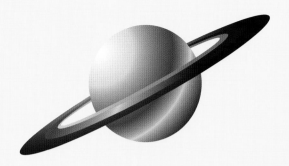

# Leap InTo Space

## Nancy F. Castaldo

### Illustrated by Patrick T. McRae

**williamsonbooks**™

Nashville, Tennessee

ISBN-13: 978-0-8249-6815-1 (hardcover)
ISBN-13: 978-0-8249-6816-8 (softcover)

Published by Williamson Books
An imprint of Ideals Publications
A Guideposts Company
535 Metroplex Drive, Suite 250
Nashville, Tennessee 37211
www.idealsbooks.com

Printed and bound in China

Library of Congress Cataloging-in-Publication Data

Castaldo, Nancy F. (Nancy Fusco), 1962-
    Kids leap into space / Nancy F. Castaldo.
        p. cm. -- (Kids can!)
    Includes bibliographical references and index.
    ISBN 978-0-8249-6816-8 (softcover : alk. paper) -- ISBN 978-0-8249-6815-1
(hardcover : alk. paper)
    1.   Outer space--Exploration--Juvenile literature. 2.   Telescopes--Juvenile
literature. 3.   Manned space flight--Juvenile literature. 4.
Astronomy--Experiments--Juvenile literature.   I. McRae, Patrick, III. II.
Title.
    QB500.22.C37 2008
    520--dc22

                                                    2007038235


10 9 8 7 6 5 4 3 2 1

**Photo Credits**

ESPENAK, FRED. Page 99, "1998 Solar Corona Composite." Copyright © 2004. Used by permission. www.MrEclipse.com.
JUPITER IMAGES: p. 57, 83. Used by permission. NATIONAL OPTICAL ASTRONOMY OBSERVATORY
(NOAO)/AURA/NSF. P. 70, "Rosette Nebula." Copyright ©. Used by permission. ROYAL OBSERVATORY EDINBURGH
(ROE)/AAO/UKS. P. 75, "Pleiades Star Cluster." Copyright ©. Used by permission. SUPERSTOCK: pages 31, 99, 77. Used
by permission. WRIGHT, EDWARD L. (Ned). P. 61, "Milky Way." Copyright ©. Used by permission. PHOTOS COURTESY
OF NASA: pages 8, 28, 31, 56, 78 & 88, 92, 114, 117; NASA Goddard Space Flight Center: p. 26; NASA Harvard-
Smithsonian Center for Astrophysics: p. 40; NASA Johnson Space Center: pages 16, 27, 107; NASA Kennedy Space Center:
p. 94; NASA, ESA, S. Beckwith (STScI) and the HUDF Team: p. 12; NASA/HST, Hubble Space Telescope: p. 24;
NASA/HST/SFPC2: p. 71; NASA/JPL, Jet Propulsion Laboratory Caltech: pages 14, 20, 33, 38, 41, 91, 109; NASA/JPL Malin
Space Science Systems: p.32; NASA/JPL NASA/JPL Northwestern University: p. 38; NASA/JPL Space Science Institute: pages
35, 91; NASA/JPL University of Arizona: p. 36; NASA/Solar & Heliospheric Observatory (SOHO)/ESA: pages 42, 55.


Project Editor: Patricia A. Pingry
Book Designer: Patrick T. McRae, McRae Studios

**Dedication**
For Dean, for giving me the moon, and Lucie, my shining star.
And for my special office buddy with the celestial blue eyes, Galileo.

My thanks go out to all of those people who encouraged, supported, and
inspired me, including Heidi Jo Newberg, Bob Berman, Joseph Rustick, teachers
Paula Ptasek, Tina Fahey, and John Kilcer; Diane Kisich Davis, Ann Terra, Pam
Wozniak, and Eric Wyckoff. As always, my gratitude to my writing buddies
(Rose Kent, Jackie Rogers, Coleen Paratore, Liza Frenette, Kyra Teis, Lois Feister
Huey, Eric Luper, and Helen Mesick), publishing sister Debbi Michiko Florence,
my family, and my unfailing professional team, Pat, Peggy, and Sara.

# Contents

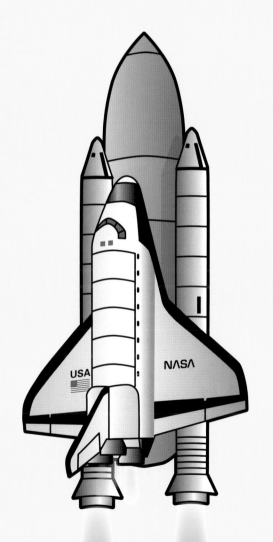

# Look Up!

**P**ick a spot outside. Lie on your back and look up at the sky. How high can you see? Can you see the top of the sky? Of course, not! There is no top. The sky seems to go on forever, doesn't it?

The sky starts right above Earth. Actually, right on top of your little toe. That's right. We don't have to get into a spaceship or an airplane to begin our leap into space. We just have to look up.

*"If you want to create an apple pie from scratch, you must first create the universe."*
**—Carl Sagan**

What do you think astronomer Carl Sagan meant when he said that in order "to create an apple pie from scratch you must first create the universe?" What role does the universe play in our lives? Probably a bigger role than you think. The apples that go into that pie grow on a tree on our planet, the Earth, and need certain things to grow, such as water, nutrients from the soil, and light from our own shining star, the sun. Everything is connected in the universe, the planets, the stars, the moons, even the apples on that tree.

## Tools of the Trade

Have you ever looked through a microscope? A *microscope* lets us see very tiny things, like cells, much larger. A *telescope* brings things closer to us that are very far away, like stars. We wouldn't have much of our knowledge of the universe without the use of telescopes. They help us see far into the sky at things that we could never see from Earth with our own eyes. There is a legend that a young Dutch boy, an apprentice to a lens maker named Hans Lippershey, accidentally invented the first telescope by looking through two lenses at the same time. He found that he could see things, like the faraway weathervane on a church, as clear as if they were near.

**Try This**

Can you invent a new product with a space-themed name? What do you want to convey with your name? Is your invention fast, "out-of-this-world" terrific, or futuristic?

## So What's an Astronomer?

An *astronomer* is a scientist who studies space, the stars, planets, and the physical universe.

**Think about It!**

## Scavenger Space Hunt

Have you ever eaten a MARS candy bar? Or driven in a Saturn car? Look around you, in school, at home, the supermarket, and at the mall, and see what else in our world has been named after planets, stars, and other things in outer space. How many did you find? Did you find Comet cleanser, Mercury cars, Pontiac Solstice car, Orion car, Milky Way candy bars, Sun Light dish detergent, Starburst candy, Ford Taurus car, Eclipse or Orbit gum, Disney's Pluto, or Skybar candy? What feeling do these names give you? Why do you think these names were picked for each product?

# Face of SPACE

## Galileo Galilei

One of the greatest astronomers was born in Italy in 1564. Galileo Galilei spent a good deal of his life questioning the accepted scientific beliefs of his time that were not proven by experiment. Galileo heard about the new Dutch instruments built to see the heavens and built one himself. He pointed his instrument into the sky and made many discoveries about the universe. He found evidence that the Earth was not at its center, just as astronomer, Nicolaus Copernicus had theorized.

His proof was found orbiting Jupiter. He found four bodies, or moons, circling that planet. It was the belief at the time that no other planet besides Earth had a moon; therefore, Earth must be the center of the universe. Galileo's findings did not sit well with the Roman Catholic Church. In 1633 he was asked to withdraw his public support of Copernicus. When he did not, he was sentenced to life imprisonment; but because he was so old, they allowed Galileo to return to his villa and live out his days under house arrest. He died in 1642.

Galileo also made many other discoveries and observations during his life. He was one of the first Europeans to observe sunspots. He was the first to report evidence of lunar mountains and craters. He also observed the Milky Way and the planet Neptune, although he did not realize that Neptune was indeed a planet and not a star.

## Collecting the Light

Telescopes are important tools for astronomers, the scientists who study space. There are refracting telescopes and reflecting telescopes. A *refracting telescope* refracts, or bends, light to produce an image. It has a large convex lens that makes objects look bigger. This lens collects the light and bends it to form an upside-down image. A *reflecting telescope* reflects the light to produce an image. It has a concave lens that collects light, then concentrates it onto a second mirror which reflects the light into the eyepiece.

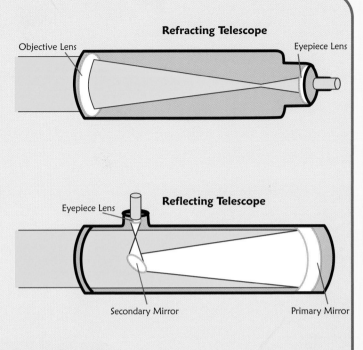

**Refracting Telescope**

Objective Lens          Eyepiece Lens

**Reflecting Telescope**

Eyepiece Lens

Secondary Mirror          Primary Mirror

## So What's Reflect & Refract?

To *reflect* means something throws back the image. To *refract* is to make the image change directions.

## So What's Convex & Concave?

Convex bulges outward. Concave is curved inward like a bowl.

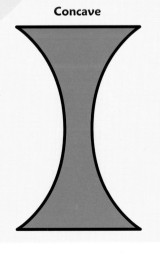

**Concave**

**Convex**

## Hubble Space Telescope

Imagine if you built a huge telescope and, instead of setting it upon a mountaintop on Earth, sent it into space. That's what the Hubble (HST), named for American astronomer Edwin Hubble, is. It is a 94.5-inch (2.4 m) telescope that spins around Earth once every ninety-seven minutes capturing enough data in its camera each day to fill an encyclopedia. The Hubble converts its images into electronic signals which are sent to a tracking satellite. They are then sent to Earth for scientists to study.

*Hubble telescope floating above Earth*

## Replacement for the Hubble

In the early 1990s the Hubble could see ten times farther than any telescope on our planet. Since that time, however, our technology has increased, and there are telescopes on Earth that compare to the Hubble. But the Hubble has the unique ability to read energy and light that does not reach Earth. The Hubble is scheduled to end its mission in 2010 after twenty years. The James Webb Space Telescope, named for a former NASA director, will replace the Hubble in 2011.

### Telescope

Here's a simple one-lens, refractive telescope that you can make. It's not much different from the early telescopes that were made to explore the night sky.

**You Need**

- Aluminum foil
- Dressmaker's straight pin
- A convex lens (look in the Resources section for information)

Make your eyepiece by stacking several layers of aluminum foil together. Next use the pin to poke through the stack. Separate the layers and see which sheet has the best small, round pinhole. Place the foil right up to your eye and look through the pinhole. Try out the different pinholes to see which one will give you the sharpest image when you look through it at a brightly lit scene.

To make your telescope, take your best pinhole and place it against your eye. Now take the lens and place it against the pinhole. Slowly and carefully move the lens away from your face until you can see a magnified scene.

Depending on how far you move your lens, the scene will either be upside-down or right side up.

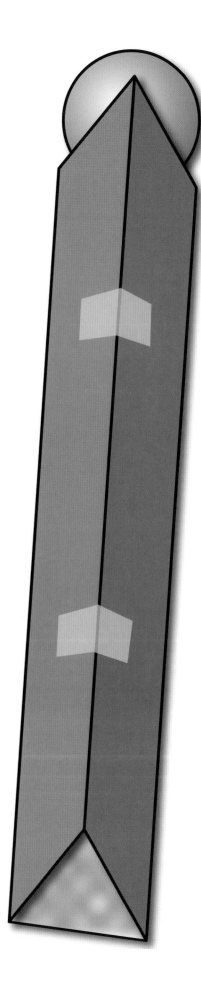

## Make It!

### Terrific Teleidoscope

What do you get when you cross a telescope with a kaleidoscope? A teleidoscope of course! A teleidoscope collects light rays and projects them down into the tube and mirrors to create multiple reflections that are as beautiful as any kaleidoscope. Here's how you can make your own.

**You Need**

- Glue stick
- Mirrored poster paper, 24 x 2 inches
- Cardboard, 24 x 2 inches
- Scissors
- Tape
- Large glass marble (optional)

Use the glue stick to glue the poster paper to the cardboard. Cut the mirrored cardboard into three pieces, each 8 x 2 inches. Align the long ends of two of the pieces and tape together. Place your tape on the cardboard side. Hold the third piece to the others with the mirrors facing inward. Observe what happens to the image when you change any of the angles in the scope.

When you have the angle you want of your scope, tape the third mirrored piece to the others forming a triangle with the mirrors inside the unit. Pick up the teleidoscope and look through it. Use stickers and markers to decorate your scope. For more fun, adhere a large glass marble to one end of your scope with tape or rubber cement. How does it change your observation?

## Distance from Earth to Proxima Centauri, the next nearest star.

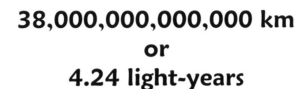

**38,000,000,000,000 km**
**or**
**4.24 light-years**

## Measuring Time and Distance

The distances in space are so vast that it's difficult to comprehend how far things really are. The numbers become so huge that it's difficult to even know how to say them out loud. The distances are beyond millions and billions and trillions of miles, so the best way to think about distances in space is to actually think about light and the time it takes light to travel to us on Earth. After all, light is what all astronomers search for in the heavens.

### Some Light-Year Distances

The Milky Way galaxy is about 150,000 light-years across.

The Andromeda galaxy is 2.3 million light-years away.

Distance from Earth to Proxima Centauri, our next nearest star, is 4.24 light-years.

## Light-Years

The sun is constantly shining, but pretend it wasn't. Let's think for a moment that the sun turned on and off like a light switch. It would take us about eight minutes to see the light after the switch was flipped on. It takes about eight minutes for the light of the sun, which is 24,000,000,000,000 miles (38,000,000,000,000 km) away to reach us.

**WOW! That's fast!**

The measurement that scientists use to measure distances in space is in *light-years*. Light travels at the speed of 186,000 miles per second (300,000 km/second), therefore a light second is 186,000 miles (300,000 km). A light-year is 5,865,696,000,000 miles (9,460,800,000,000 km) or the amount light travels in one Earth year, close to *6 trillion miles*.

## Black as Night?

Do you ever wonder why the night sky is not filled with light if so many bright stars are shining above? Astronomers have asked the same question. Wilhelm Olbers, a nineteenth-century astronomer, thought about the brightness of the night sky for years. The question of why the night sky is black became known as *Olbers' paradox*.

Olbers believed that the night sky is dark because the dust in space absorbs the light of the stars. Unfortunately, later scientists discovered that if that were the case, the stars would heat up the dust and the sky would glow, creating light. The question was still unanswered.

Astronomer Edward Harrison, author of *Darkness at Night: A Riddle of the Universe*, claims there simply aren't enough stars to cover the sky with light, but many scientists believe that there are an immeasurable number of stars in an infinitely large cosmos, or universe. It's just that you can't see them all.

*The Hubble Ultra Deep Field*

## Think about It!

The stars we see in the night sky look like sparkling white diamonds. Is the light from our own star, the sun, also white? We turn on a light bulb and the light it emits looks white, but is it?

### So What's a Cosmos?

When we speak of the total universe, we use the word cosmos.

## Science Speak

Scientists use instruments called *spectrographs* to separate light into the different colors. Astronomers use the spectrograph to look at the color of stars. The spectrograph shows the star's range of color. When astronomers look at the spectrum of a star with the spectrograph they look for identifiable lines that depict the signature of the elements that the star is made of, such as calcium. Each element absorbs light at a different frequency, leaving a dark line in the star's spectrum.

## EXPERIMENT

### Experiment with a Rainbow Star

Use a prism to separate the light and see the different colors. The rainbow we see using the prism is the spectrum of our star, the sun.

**You Need**

- Flashlight
- Prism
- White paper

Shine the light of the flashlight through the prism onto the paper. What do you see? Try holding the prism up to a window. Is the sunlight really white?

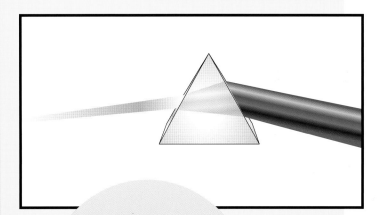

### So What's a Spectrum?
A *spectrum* is a range of colors that make up light.

### Roy G. Biv

Let me introduce Roy G. Biv. He's not some famous astronaut; he's simply a mnemonic device for helping you remember the colors of the spectrum. Each letter represents the first letter in a color: Red, Orange, Yellow, Green, Blue, Indigo, Violet. Look at a rainbow and you'll see the colors in that order.

# Our Neighborhood

**W**e live on planet Earth. Our planet is not alone in the universe; it's one of thousands or millions of planets and stars in space. Earth is one of the eight planets that rotate or orbit around our star we call the *sun*. Together the sun and the planets make up our own neighborhood in space, called the *solar system*.

*Photo: A comparison of the sizes and distances of the planets in our solar system*

Sun

Mercury

Venus

Earth

Mars

Jupiter

Saturn

Uranus

Neptune

Pluto

# Try This ↓

## Silly Solar Sayings

In order from the sun, the planets in our solar system are Mercury, Venus, Earth, Mars, Jupiter, Saturn. Uranus, Neptune. You can remember this order with a silly sentence using the first letters of each of the planet names, "**M**y **V**ery **E**xcellent **M**other **J**ust **S**ent **U**s **N**ets" or "**M**om's **V**ery **E**xpensive **M**otorcycle **J**ust **S**ped **U**p **N**ebraska." Make your own silly solar saying using the first letters of the planet names. Here's how.

**You Need**

• Paper and pencil

Write down the names of the planets in order from the sun. Take each first letter of the planets and think of another word that starts with that letter. List them underneath each planet name. Use your list of words to make a silly solar sentence. Share your silly saying with your friends and see whose is the silliest. Test yourself the next day and see if you can remember the order of the planets using your sentence to help you.

My Very Excited Mouse Just Swam Under Niagra!

## So What's a Planet?

A *planet* is generally defined as a body that reflects the light of the star it orbits.

# The Atmosphere

## The Troposphere

The Earth has a thin layer of gases that protects us from the heat or radiation from the sun. It's called the *atmosphere*. Picture one of those sand art jars with the different colors of sand layered on top of each other. Our atmosphere is layered just like that. The bottom layer of sand or first layer of our atmosphere beginning right above your toe is called the *troposphere*. It's filled with the air around us. It's where there are clouds and our weather happens.

## The Stratosphere

The next layer is the *stratosphere*. It begins at the top of the troposphere and extends upward for about fifty miles (80.47 km). There is virtually no weather in this layer, which makes it the perfect layer for commercial airplanes. If you've flown in a plane, you've probably flown in the lower part of the stratosphere where there is little turbulence.

## So What's an Atmosphere?

We use the word *atmosphere* to include all of the layers of gases—the air—that surround the planets.

*An aurora seen from the space shuttle*

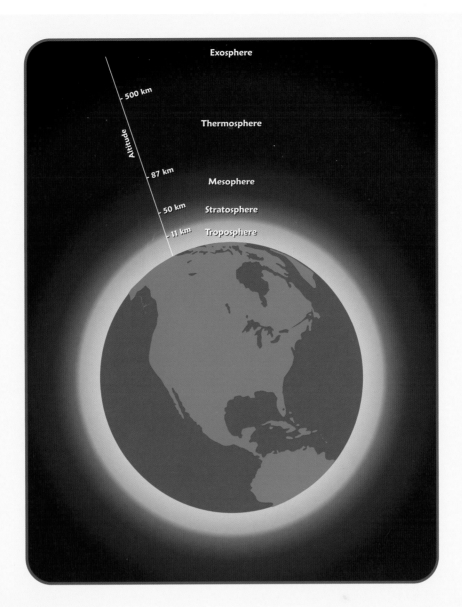

## The Mesophere, Thermosphere, and Ionosphere

Meteors burn up in the next layer, the *mesosphere*. The *thermosphere*, the layer above the mesosphere, is the layer where the space shuttle orbits the Earth. The *ionosphere* isn't actually another layer, but is part of the thermosphere. Although it's a very thin layer, it is important because this is where the sun's energy is able to break apart molecules and long distance radio communication is possible. It is also the part of the atmosphere where there are *auroras* (see page 57) or northern lights.

## The Exosphere

The last layer of our atmosphere is the *exosphere*. This is where our atmosphere merges with space or what is called *dark sky*.

# Make It!

## Weather Station Express

You can set up your own backyard weather station to record the happenings in the troposphere where you live. Here's how.

**You Need**

- Poster board
- Markers
- Ruler
- Outdoor thermometer to record temperature
- A rain gauge to record rainfall
- Weathervane to record the direction of the wind

Make a weather calendar first to record your station results. Draw a monthly calendar on a sheet of poster board (draw seven boxes horizontally and five boxes vertically). Hang the calendar where you can write on it each day. Hang the thermometer outside your window. Place the rain gauge and the weathervane in a spot that you can visit each day. At the same time each day look at your instruments. Record on your calendar square for that day the temperature, wind direction, and amount of rainfall. Draw a sun, cloud, or rain to show what the day was like. At the end of the month, count how many days it was sunny and how many days it rained. What was the highest temperature? What other observations did you notice?

## Try This ⬇

Make a sand art jar with different colors of sand to represent the different layers of our atmosphere. Draw a picture of what the layers look like above the earth. What layer is on the bottom? Draw a rain cloud in the troposphere. Draw an airplane in the stratosphere. Draw a space shuttle in the next layer. Can you remember all of the layers from the Earth to space? What else can you draw in the upper layers?

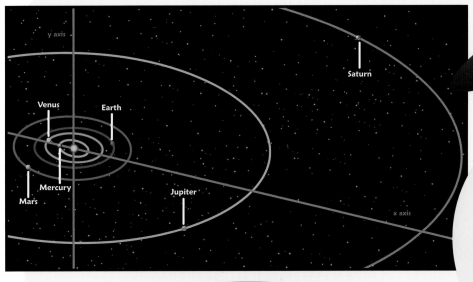

So What's an Ellipse?

An *ellipse* is something that is in the shape of an oval. *Elliptical* means something is in the shape of an ellipse.

# EXPERIMENT

## Experiment with Excellent Ellipses

Planet orbits are elliptical. There are two fixed points on either side of the ellipse called *foci*. In any planet orbit one point, or foci, is the sun. Does the distance between the two points matter to the shape of the ellipse? Find out how the distance relates to the planet orbit in this simple experiment.

### You Need

- 2 thumbtacks
- Cardboard
- Ruler
- String
- Pencil

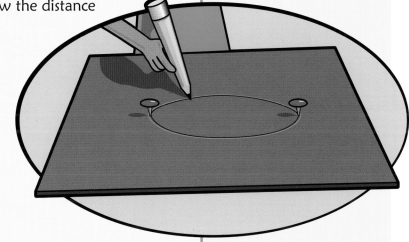

Stick two thumbtacks into the cardboard about four inches (10 cm) apart. Wind a twelve-inch (30-cm) string around the thumbtacks and tie the ends together. Place a sharpened pencil inside the string and trace the ellipse. Remember to keep the string tight. Repeat the process, but place the thumbtacks closer together about two inches (5 cm) apart. Compare the shapes that result. Does the distance between the foci affect the ellipse's shape?

# Innies and Outies

No, this isn't about belly buttons. Planets are divided into two categories, the *inner planets* and the *outer planets*. Inner planets, or innies, are relatively small, closest to the sun, and made mostly of rock. These planets are Mercury, Venus, Earth, and Mars.

The outer planets are much larger, mostly made of gas, and have many circling bodies, called *moons*. They are also much farther away from the sun. The farther the planet is from the sun the less heat reaches it and the cooler it is. These outer planets are Jupiter, Saturn, Uranus, and Neptune.

*A montage of the planets taken by spacecraft that have visited them*

## Make It!

### A Planet Mobile

Using pictures of the planets from National Aeronautics and Space Administration (NASA) you can create your own solar system mobile to hang in your room. Here's how.

**You Need**

- Computer
- Printer
- Scissors
- Glue stick
- Yellow sturdy paper plate
- Hole punch
- String

Log onto the NASA site at **www.nasa.gov/audience/forkids/ activities/A_Planet_Cutouts.html** and print out two copies of the planet pictures. Cut out the planet pictures and glue together the two sides of each. Cut a zigzag border on the paper plate to create the sun. To put your mobile together, you need to punch a small hole at the top of each planet and tie a length of string around each hole. Punch holes in the sun along the edges and tie the dangling planets to the sun in their planet order. Attach another string to the top of the mobile to hang it up.

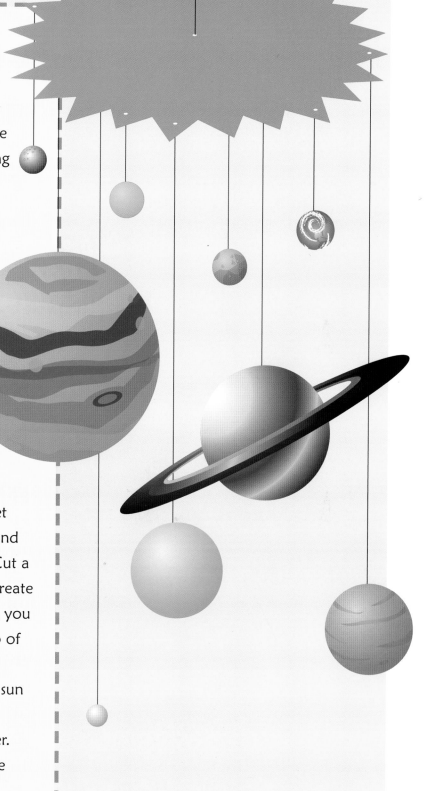

## Days and Nights

A *day* is the time it takes for a planet to rotate on its *axis*, the imaginary line passing through the Earth from the North Pole to the South Pole (360°). A *year* is measured by the time is takes for a planet to make one revolution of the sun.

An Earth day is about twenty-four hours long. How long do you think a day on another planet is? The planet with the shortest day is Jupiter. It takes Jupiter only 9.8 Earth hours to turn on its axis. Venus has the longest day. It takes Venus 243 Earth days to complete one rotation. That's a long day! The funny thing is that, although it takes Venus so long to make one rotation, it takes Venus only 224.7 Earth days to revolve around the sun. So that makes a day on Venus longer than a year on Venus.

### So What's an Axis?

An *axis* is an imaginary straight line that passes through a solid object and around which the object rotates.

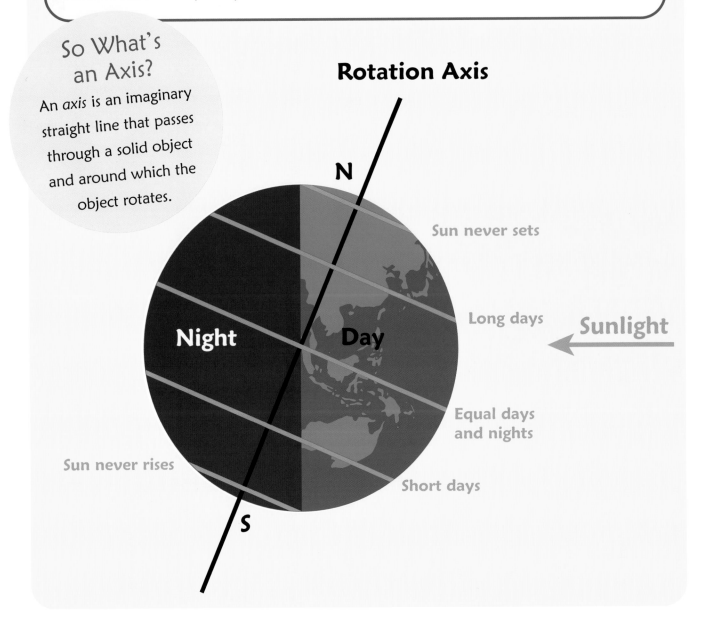

**Rotation Axis**

N

Night

Day

Sun never sets

Long days

**Sunlight**

Equal days and nights

Short days

Sun never rises

S

## Planets in Our Solar System

| Planet | Distance from Sun | Planet Year (in Earth days) | Planet Day (in Earth hours) |
|---|---|---|---|
| Mercury | 36 million miles (57.9 million km) | 87.96 days | 58.7 Earth days |
| Venus | 67.2 million miles (108.2 million km) | 224.68 days | 243 Earth days |
| Earth | 93 million miles (149.6 million km) | 365.26 days | 24 hours |
| Mars | 141.6 million miles (227.9 million km) | 686.98 days | 24.6 hours |
| Jupiter | 483.6 million miles (778.3 million km) | 11.862 Earth years | 9.84 hours |
| Saturn | 886.7 million miles (1,427 million km) | 29.456 Earth years | 10.2 hours |
| Uranus | 1,784 million miles (2,871 million km) | 84.07 Earth years | 17.9 hours |
| Neptune | 2,794.4 million miles (4,497 million km) | 164.81 Earth years | 19.1 hours |

## Think about It!

Since a day on Venus is equal to 243 of our days on Earth, what kind of a calendar could you develop for the planet Venus? What would you do if you lived on a planet with a very short day, like Jupiter, that is fewer than ten hours long? When would you sleep and for how long? How long would your school day be?

## Goofy Pluto

There was a time when Pluto was considered the ninth planet in our solar system. Not anymore. In 2006, the International Astronomical Union took Pluto off the roster. It's not that the Union didn't like Pluto; Pluto doesn't conform to the Union's definition of a planet.

Pluto was discovered in 1930. It was believed that it was a medium-sized planet like Earth and was added to our list of planets. Much later it was found to be very small, much smaller than previously believed, so small that it is tinier than many moons in the solar system, including Earth's. If the Union decided to keep Pluto on the roster, they would have to declare a few other tiny bodies, Xena, Ceres, and Charon, proper planets, bringing the number of planets in our solar system up to twelve. The Union made the decision to downgrade Pluto to dwarf planet status, reducing the number of proper planets in our solar system to eight.

*Pluto and its moon Charon, as seen from the Hubble telescope*

## Naming Pluto

How would you like to actually name a planet? Venetia Burney, an eleven-year-old from Oxford, England, did just that in 1930 when Planet X was discovered. She researched the names of Greek gods and found Pluto, the god of the dark and distant underworld. The planet that was discovered was so far from the sun that she thought Pluto was the perfect name for it. Her father sent a telegram to the Arizona observatory and on May 1, 1930, Planet X was officially named Pluto.

# Try This ↓

If you were eight Earth years old, how old would you be if you lived on Mars? Or Mercury? Let's try and figure it out.

**You Need**

- Calculator
- Pencil
- Notepad

Let's convert your age into days instead of years. Multiply your age by 365.26 days because that's how many days we have in one Earth year. Write that number down on your notepad. That is the number of days you have been alive on Earth. Now find out how many Mars years you have lived by dividing that number by 686.98, which is the number of Earth days in a Mars year. Your answer would be your age on Mars. You can use the same method to find out your age on the other planets in our solar system. Look at the chart on page 23 to find out the number of Earth days in the planet year. Surprise your parents by telling them their ages on Mars; they'll feel a lot younger. Which planets will make them feel a lot older?

# Hunt for Another Earth

For hundreds of years astronomers have wondered if there were other planets out there, like Earth, that have conditions favorable to life. This speculation was not always good for the astronomer. For instance, Giordano Bruno, an Italian monk, was burned at the stake in 1600 for speaking about life on other planets. And Galileo was convinced that alien beings lived on the planet Jupiter. But for the most part, scientists have been able to see only giant planets—which are mostly gas balls—orbiting distant stars.

In June of 2005 a team of astronomers in Hawaii located a planet roughly 7.5 times the mass of our planet circling a dim red star, Gliese 876, in the constellation Aquarius. Scientists determined that this planet is made of rock and ice rather than gas, making it fall between the composition of Earth and Uranus. It is, however, so close to its sun that it would be too hot to support life. But the discovery of a planet that is similar to ours in many ways encourages scientists in their search for other planets that might sustain life.

*Gliese 876*

## View from Space

*"The stars don't look bigger, but they do look brighter."*
—*Sally Ride*

Astronaut Sally Ride talked about her views while in space. What would you see if you looked at Earth from space? According to the astronauts of NASA they can see where the snow lines stop and the land is green again. They can see storms and cold fronts in the atmosphere very clearly.

*Astronaut Sally Ride*

## Planet Just Discovered

The Daily Globe

**Planet Just Discovered**

Ouch! That's hot!

In 2006 astronomers discovered a new planet outside our solar system. They named it SWEEPS-10, a perfect name, because this planet is the fastest known planet. It has a "year" of only ten hours long. The following year a planet orbiting a star in the constellation Hercules was found to be a gas giant, similar to Jupiter in size and nature, except this planet is a hot 3,700°F. The planet has been named HD 149026b and is 279 light-years away from Earth.

# Weigh In

It's time to weigh in and see how your weight on Earth compares with your weight on other planets. That's where gravity comes in. Your weight is a measurement of the force of attraction between you and the Earth or any other planet. The force of gravity depends on two things; the mass, or size, of the planet and your mass. If you double your mass, gravity will pull on you twice as hard. If the planet you are standing on is twice as large, gravity also pulls on you twice as hard, and you will have a different weight.

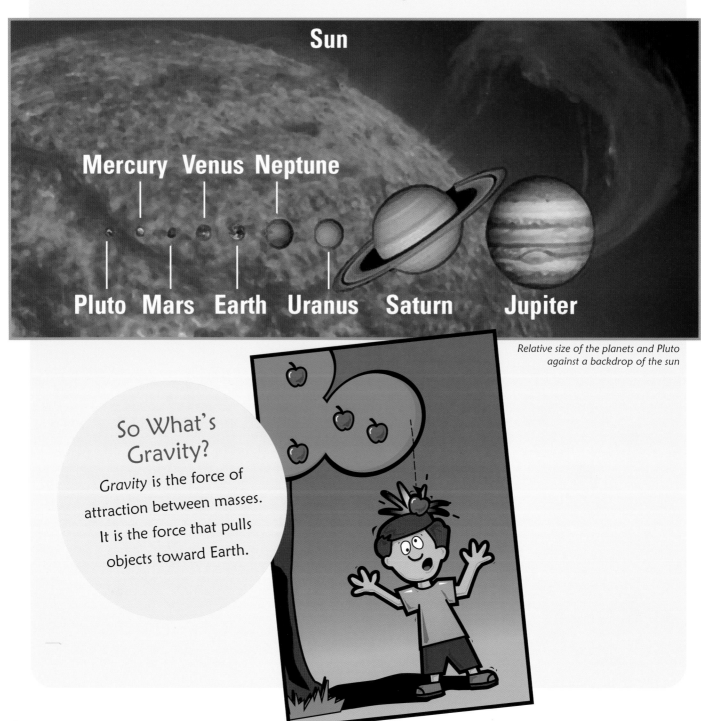

Relative size of the planets and Pluto against a backdrop of the sun

## So What's Gravity?

*Gravity* is the force of attraction between masses. It is the force that pulls objects toward Earth.

# Try This ↓

## Guess Your Weight on Other Planets

### You Need

- Scale
- Paper
- Pencil
- Computer

Weigh yourself on the scale and take a look at the size of the Earth in the picture. Record your weight.

Take a look at Mercury. Is Mercury smaller or larger than the Earth? Is it made of rock material or gases? Would it have a large mass or a small mass? Do you think you would weigh more or less on Mercury? Take a guess and record it on the paper.

Take a look at the next planet. Again, is it smaller or larger than Earth? What is it made of? Take a guess on what your weight would be on that planet. More or less? Do the same for all the planets.

Now it is time to check your answers and see how close you came to the actual weights. Log onto Your Weight on Other Worlds at **www.exploratorium.edu/ronh/weight/**. (Here's another site to try **www.onlineconversion.com/weight_on_other_planets.htm**)

Note your weight in the box and hit CALCULATE. You'll see under each planet the weight you would be if you were standing on that planet.

How close were your guesses? Did a planet like Jupiter fool you? You may have thought that you would weigh a lot more on Jupiter because it is so large, but Jupiter is a gaseous planet, so it has a small mass. You actually weigh less.

## Nicolaus Copernicus

Nicolaus Copernicus was born in Poland in 1473. When he was growing up, people believed that the Earth was the center of our universe. This belief was known as the traditional *geocentric theory.*

Young Nicolaus went to the university and then on to Rome where he could observe a lunar eclipse. (A *lunar eclipse* happens when the Earth obscures the sun from the moon's point of view. You can learn more about these eclipses in Chapter 7.) In 1514, Copernicus wrote a commentary about his theory that the sun was the center and not the Earth. His *heliotropic theory* stated that the Earth was another planet, that it circled the sun once a year, and that it turned on its axis once a day. This theory also explained the different seasons on Earth. His theory was not widely accepted, but it has been proven to be true.

### Think about It!

Check out the days of the week and the names of the months, and you'll see that the heavens have had an impact on our calendar. In ancient Rome the days were named for Roman gods and goddesses such as *dies Lunae* for the goddess Luna and *dies Martis* for the god Mars. Our modern names for these two days are Monday and Tuesday, but in Spanish they are *Lunes* and *Martes,* a little closer sounding to the original names.

# Mars

Astronaut Buzz Aldrin was quoted as saying, "I think humans will reach Mars, and I would like to see it happen in my lifetime." We have not reached that

*Astronaut Edwin (Buzz) Aldrin on the moon, July 20, 1969*

milestone yet, but we are getting much closer. The first successful mission to Mars occurred in 1999 with the Surveyor that orbited the planet for more than seven years and provided NASA with maps of the Red Planet. Since then rovers have landed on the surface of the planet and provided scientists with a great deal of information, including the discovery that liquid water once existed on the planet surface.

Mars is the closest planet to Earth. We know many things about Mars, but there is still much more to learn. We know that it is a rocky planet and, like

Earth, has been changed by its volcanoes, the movement of its crust, impacts from objects colliding with it in space, and its atmosphere. Unlike Earth, which has shifting tectonic plates that move side to side to cause earthquakes, Mars has a crust that shifts up and down, with hot lava moving up through the crust.

At times the whole planet becomes engulfed in great dust storms. Because of this, there are huge sand dunes and wind-shaped features that can be seen.

The Mars Reconnaissance Orbiter is the latest in the program. It will track changes in the dust and water in the atmosphere of Mars and look for more evidence of the planet's climate changes and the water that once existed on the surface.

Will humans reach Mars? It's likely. When? We'll have to wait and see.

*A simulation of the Mars Rover descending into Victoria Crater*

*Mars as seen from the Mars Global Surveyor*

## Another Name for Antigravity

If gravity is a force that pulls objects together, can you imagine a force that pushes them apart? Scientists know the mysterious force pushing the universe apart at a fast rate as *dark energy.*

# This Just In

Every day there are new discoveries and new developments in the space program. We've seen that the two Mars rovers, Spirit and Opportunity, have been successful, but they do have their limitations. They have only been able to cover ten square miles and cannot collect data more than a few feet off the ground. Enter Archimedes, a balloon craft, which will hover close to the planet's surface, allowing for clear photographs to be taken. Archimedes, funded by the private German Mars Society, will reach Mars in 2009. Look for more news on Archimedes in the coming years.

*Archimedes inflated*

*The Twin Peaks on Mars*

# Face of SPACE

## Sir Isaac Newton

Sir Isaac Newton was born in England in 1643 and died in 1727. During his lifetime he was a physicist, mathematician, alchemist, inventor, philosopher, and astronomer. Have you heard the story of the apple falling on Newton's head and his discovery of gravity? Well, Newton did not have an apple fall on his head. He did, however, come up with the idea that the power of gravity, which could bring an apple down from a tree, was not limited to a certain distance from Earth but must extend farther than what was originally thought. He went on to propose that this gravity could extend all the way to the moon and must influence the moon's orbit.

## Experiment with Motion Commotion

Did you ever wonder why the planets don't spin out of the solar system? Scientist Sir Isaac Newton determined that a planet's motion around the sun is a result of gravity and inertia. Inertia is a property of matter that causes the planet to resist changes in speed or direction. Here's a simple experiment that demonstrates this property.

### You Need

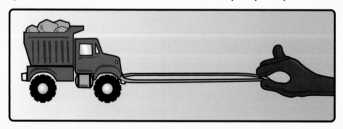

- Rubber band
- Toy dump truck
- Rocks

Attach the rubber band to the front of the truck. Fill the truck with rocks. Pull on the rubber band until truck starts to move. How much does the rubber band need to stretch in order for the truck to move? Continue pulling. Does the rubber band stretch more or less once the truck is moving?

# Jupiter

Take a look into the night sky on a summer night, and you're bound to see Jupiter shining brightly in the sky. In fact, Jupiter is just about the brightest light in the sky. It is a super-sized planet with a mass greater than all the other planets combined and then doubled! According to astronomer Bob Berman, Jupiter could "swallow 1,400 Earths." The most recognizable feature on the planet is a great big spot, which is appropriately called the Great Red Spot. It's not actually a spot like on a dalmatian; it's really a huge hurricane that is twice the size of Earth with a color that is sort of reddish-pink. It's so large that we can see it with a telescope. There are other storms on Jupiter as well, but none quite as large and not all of them reddish-pink in color.

*Cassini spacecraft photograph of Jupiter*

# The Rings of Saturn

Saturn, named after the Roman god of agriculture, is not the only planet with rings circling it; but the ring system of Saturn is unique. Galileo described them as "handles" and first saw them in the early seventeenth century with his twenty-power telescope. He said, "I have observed the highest planet to be tripled-bodied. This is to say that to my very great amazement Saturn was seen to me to be not a single star, but three together, which almost touch each other."

*Saturn*

# A Triple Planet?

Two of Saturn's rings are bright and the third ring is a bit fainter. The third ring was discovered in 1850 and is often referred to as the Dusky Ring. These rings are the reason that, initially, Saturn was thought to be a triple planet. The intricate rings are made of ice chunks and rocks that range from the size of a kernel of corn to that of a car and are visible to us only with a telescope.

We have many beautiful photos of Saturn's rings, and scientists have learned more about their structure from the various missions to Saturn. NASA's

Pioneer 11 was the first spacecraft to visit Saturn in 1979, followed by Voyager I and Voyager II. Cassini arrived at Saturn in 2004 and is a joint project between NASA and ESA, the European Space Agency. Cassini will orbit Saturn for at least four years. Who knows what other discoveries will be made? (You can find out what Cassini discovered about Saturn's moon on page 91.)

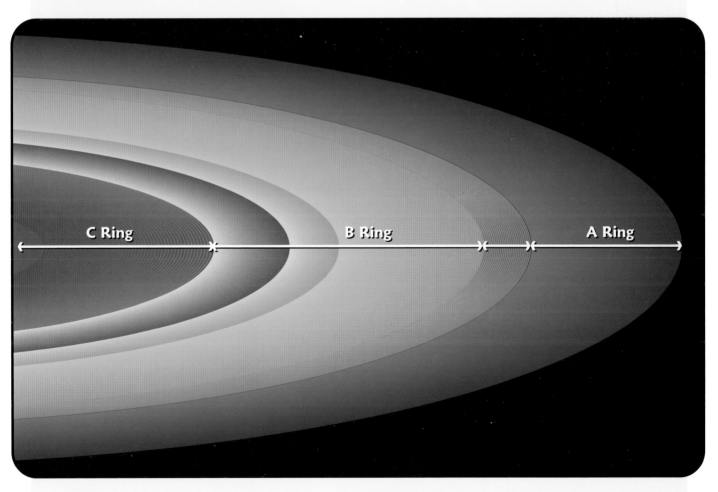

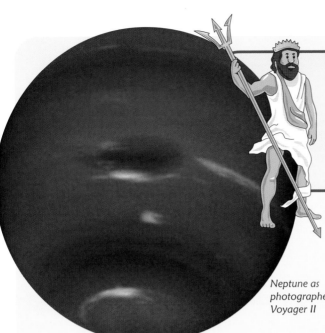

## Neptune

The blue planet of Neptune was named after the Roman god of the sea. Its Great Dark Spot at the center of the planet is as long as the Earth is wide.

*Neptune as photographed by Voyager II*

## Venus

Venus is similar to Earth in size, mass, composition, and distance from the Sun. But Venus has no ocean and is covered by thick, rapidly spinning clouds that trap heat and create a greenhouse-like world. Temperatures are hot enough to melt lead.

*Venus as seen from the Magellan spacecraft*

## Try This ⬇

Venus is most visible in the sky just after sunset and just after sunrise. See if you can find it!

## Mercury

The closest planet to the sun was named after Mercury, the messenger to the Roman gods. Mercury is so swift that it moves on its orbit at about one-and-one-half times the speed of Earth, but it spins very slowly on its axis—so slowly that six Earth months pass before one day on Mercury.

*Mercury as seen from Mariner 10 spacecraft*

# Try This ↓

## Name the Planet

Here's a fun game to test your knowledge of the planets. Play it with your friends and see who will be the planet champion.

**You Need**

- 8 index cards
- Pen
- Group of 4 or so friends

Write down everything you know about each planet on each of the index cards. Pretend you are the planet when you write your description. Describe yourself. For example: I am sometimes called the Red Planet. I am the fourth planet from the sun. I have a connection to the day Tuesday.

Write a card for each planet. Invite your friends to play your game. Read each of the cards aloud to your friends and see if they can guess which planet you are describing. Did you guess the planet Mars in the description above?

## Deep Sky

What lies beyond our solar system neighborhood? We know there are other stars and other galaxies and other planets. In between is invisible stuff called *dark matter*. Scientists refer to the area outside our solar system as *deep sky*. It's where we're now headed, into the stars and other galaxies outside of our own neighborhood.

# Brown Dwarfs

Pretend you're an astronomer and you're looking at bodies in the universe that sort of look and act like planets by orbiting around stars, but they also act a bit like stars by giving off their own light. *Hmmm.* What do you do with this information? Scientists are always confronted with new discoveries in space that challenge their theories and view of the universe. Over the past decade, astronomers have found these bodies that don't conform to their definition of a planet or a star. They call them *brown dwarfs.*

The brown dwarfs shine like weak stars but quickly start to cool down like planets and stop shining. These dwarfs float around the galaxy independently, like stars, but there are some that orbit around stars, like planets. Scientists have found hundreds of brown dwarfs. Some are young and are found in star-forming regions, and others are older and in the neighborhood of our own solar system.

*A swarm of newborn brown dwarfs uncovered by NASA's Hubble Space Telescope.*

## Milestone

The first brown dwarf was discovered in 1995. It was named Gliese 229B and is located in the constellation Lepus, about 19 light-years from Earth. It has a mass of twenty to fifty times that of Jupiter, which would ordinarily make it too massive to be classified as a planet and closer in size to a star. It does, however, orbit a red dwarf star, just as a planet would.

*The star Gliese 229 (left) and a companion brown dwarf 229B (right)*

**WOW! That's huge!**

### Here Comes the Sun!

Let's take a closer look at just what a star is, and what better way to begin than with our own star, the sun? The sun, unlike the other stars that light up our nights, lights up our days. It is the center of our solar system and our next discovery.

# Life-Giving Sun

Good Morning, Sunshine. Earth says hello! The sun, our very own star, greets us each day. We depend on it for so much. It warms the Earth, fuels the plants on our planet through the process of photosynthesis, and provides us with important energy. It is proven that in areas that lack sunlight for long periods of time, there is a higher rate of sadness. We need the sun. It not only powers our planet, but it powers us along with it! Let's take a look at our own shining star.

### Telling Time

Who needs a watch when you have the sun? A sundial lets us witness the Earth's revolution and keeps time for us. It is the oldest known time-telling device and the most ancient scientific instrument. The sundial is based on shadows caused by the sun that move from one side of an object to the other side of the object over time.

We see the sun rising in the east and setting in the west. It seems as if the sun is moving across the sky during the day, but actually we are the ones moving. The movement we see is actually the Earth rotating. It makes the sun seem like it's moving across the sky and it makes shadows change their position.

### The Shining Sun

Not only is the sun the largest object in our solar system, it's so much bigger than anything else, that Earth is just a dot compared with it. The sun is a giant ball of gas that is about 70% hydrogen gas and about 28% helium. These percentages change over time as the hydrogen atoms combine to form helium atoms in a process called *fusion*. Fusion releases energy. The energy is in the form of light and heat. It's what makes the sun shine and what makes us warm.

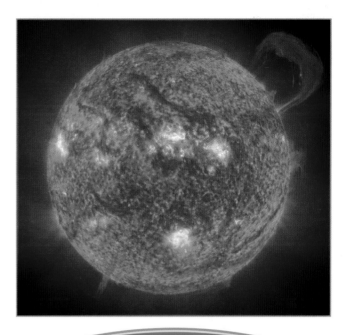

## EXPERIMENT

### Experiment with Rad Rays

The sun is glowing 93 million miles away and yet we can feel the sun's warming rays every time we step outside on a sunny day. Here's a way that you can prove the sun really does warm the Earth.

**You Need**
- 2 shallow bowls
- Water
- Thermometer

Fill each of the bowls with an inch of cold water. Place one bowl outside in direct sunlight. Place the other in the shade. Take the temperature of each bowl when you set them out. After one hour check the water temperature again in each of the bowls. Are they the same? How did their temperatures change?

*The sun as seen in an Extreme Ultraviolet Imaging Telescope (EIT) image. The hottest areas appear almost white, while the darker red areas indicate cooler temperatures.*

# Make It!

## Simple Sundial

Make this simple sundial and you might not need to wear a watch anymore, or will you?

**You Need**

- Paper plate
- 8-inch stick
- Markers
- Ruler
- A clock or watch
- Thumbtacks

Bring the paper plate outside on a sunny day and place it on the ground. Poke the stick through the center. Use the ruler to draw a line from the stick to the outside of the plate. Slant the stick toward the line and toward the rim of the plate. Go outside at noon (1:00 PM if you are on daylight savings time) and turn the plate so that the shadow of the stick falls right along the line you drew. Tack the plate to the ground so that the wind won't move it. Visit the sundial at 1:00 PM and at 2:00 PM to check the position of the shadow on the plate. Mark the position and write the time next to it. Use the ruler to draw lines from the stick to each mark. Put the clock away and visit the sundial later in the day. Can you guess what time it is by the shadow on the dial?

Check your watch to see if you are close. Visit the sundial on another sunny day to tell the time. What do you think happens on a cloudy day? Will you still be able to use your sundial?

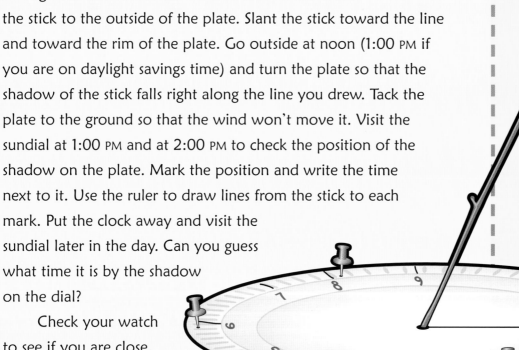

## The Longitude Dial

William Andrews, noted timepiece authority, has developed a different kind of sundial he calls a Longitude Dial. It tells time just like a sundial, but it also tells place. The shadow cast by the sun travels across a map etched into the base of the dial by a laser. When the gold-plated bead wire throws a small round shadow on the map, you can see exactly the place where the sun is precisely overhead.

## Early Sundial

The Egyptians created very precise sundials. An example from 800 BC was made from a rock called *green schist*. The sundial has a straight base with a crosspiece at one end, an east-west inscription, and measurements to show time increments. The shadow of the crosspiece on the base indicates the time.

6th Hour (Noon)
5th Hour
4th Hour
3rd Hour
2nd Hour
1st Hour (Sunrise)

## Make It!

### Sun God Bookmark

The ancient Egyptians created symbols of their gods. Here's how you can use a symbol of Ra to make a bookmark for your favorite book.

**You Need**

- White cardstock (2 x 6 inches)
- Colored pencils
- Clear contact paper
- Scissors
- Hole punch
- Yellow ribbon

Scarab

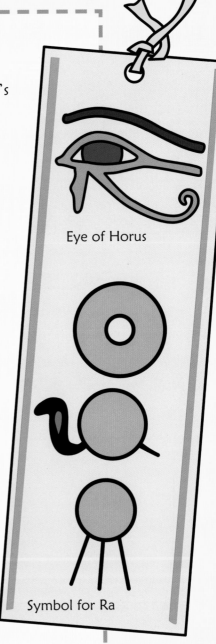

Eye of Horus

Symbol for Ra

Pick out one of the symbols for your bookmark. The symbol made up of three circles is designed to show the sun god, Ra, holding the ankh symbols in his arms. The ankh symbolized eternal life. The winged sun disk symbol was very common among the Egyptians. Ra was called the Sun of Righteousness with healing in his wings. This symbol was carved over the doorways of many temples and tombs. Draw one of the symbols on your cardstock and color it in with the colored pencils. Cover your finished design with clear contact paper and trim the edges with your scissors. Punch a small hole at the top of your bookmark and attach a piece of yellow ribbon to finish off your bookmark.

Winged Disk

Ankh

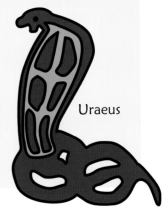

Uraeus

## Ra, the Egyptian Sun God

If you look carefully at most Egyptian art, you'll see a man shown with a falcon's head wearing a sun disk. He's often seen in a little boat crossing the sky. This is the Egyptian sun god, Ra.

The Egyptians believed that every morning Ra woke up, took a bath in the Sea of Heaven, and got in his shiny sun boat to sail across the sky. Each hour the people watched his boat move across the sky from east to west; but when night approached, Ra steered his boat below the horizon. There, Ra entered the Underworld and had to fight the serpent monster, Apep. Every night Apep waited to devour Ra and his shiny boat, and each night Ra fought for his life. Once out of danger Ra would sail safely out of the Underworld and return to the eastern sky to begin his journey once again.

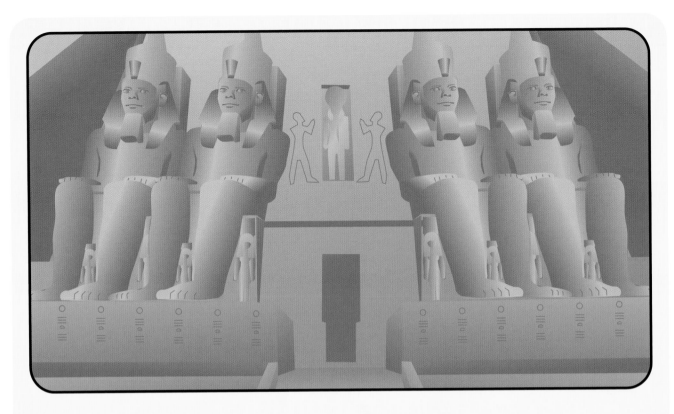

## Egyptian Temple

The Temple of Ramses II (The Great) at Abu Simbel in Egypt was built to honor Ramses' beautiful wife Nefertari. The Egyptians engineered the temple in such a way so that at daybreak twice a year—on the Pharoah's birthday and his coronation (February 22 and October 22)—a shaft of sunlight passes through the temple corridor and illuminates an altar where the golden statues of Ramses II and three other gods are situated.

This spectacle has lasted over 3,200 years even after the Nasser Dam was built and many temples were flooded. This temple, along with another, was moved to higher ground before the dam was operational. When the Egyptians moved the temples, they had the gigantic figures of Ramses carved out of the mountain at the front of the temple, cut up and then reconfigured so that the engineering of the ancient Egyptians remained intact.

People still flock to the temple at sunrise, but now on February 21 and October 21, to see the sun illuminate the darkened altar. What an awesome sight!

## Try This ⬇

### Create Your Own Gift Cards

There are many light-sensitive papers that you can purchase in a craft store. These papers react when they are exposed to light, and you can create pictures with them in the same way as in the experiment on the next page. Create your own gift cards with a little help from a star!

# In the Beginning: A Sun Legend from Australia

In the beginning, before there were men on Earth, there was no sun. There were only stars and the moon. One day the emu Dinewan and his friend Brolga were arguing and fighting. Brolga got so angry she ran to the emu's nest, picked up one of the large eggs, and threw it with all her might into the sky. The egg burst open and the yellow yolk lighted a pile of firewood. The world had never seen such light.

A good spirit saw the light and how lovely the earth looked all lit up. From that time on, the good spirit and his attendants gather wood and light a huge fire, but before they set it ablaze they send the morning star to alert everyone on Earth that the fire will soon be lit.

# EXPERIMENT

## Experiment with Sun Prints

Sunlight can fade colors. You might have noticed this on curtains, couch cushions, or artwork near a sunny window. You might not know that you can use sunlight's fading powers to create your own pictures. Here's how.

**You Need**

- Objects such as leaves, toys, flowers, and cookie cutters
- Construction paper (dark colors)

Arrange the objects on the construction paper in a design you like. Place the paper and objects in the bright sun. Don't move the objects for at least one hour. During that time the sun will fade the paper and you will see the design you have created. It will look like a silhouette of the objects.

*The total solar eclipse on February 26, 1998, © by Fred Espenak*

## The Solar Eclipse

Have you ever experienced a *solar eclipse?* A solar eclipse occurs when the moon comes directly between Earth and the sun and temporarily totally or partially blocks out the sun. Let's imagine you're watching a solar eclipse. It gets darker as the moon moves in front of the sun. Eventually the moon completely covers the sun and the day becomes as dark as night. You don't feel the heat of the sun and the air begins to cool. It's quiet. Then, slowly, the moon moves away from the sun and daylight returns.

For people living a long time ago, this was a frightening experience because they didn't have the scientific knowledge to explain things. The word *eclipse*, Greek for "abandonment," describes exactly how these early people felt when they saw their daylight disappear. Ancient China was one of many cultures which believed that during the eclipse, the sun was being eaten by a dragon. The people would make lots of noise during an eclipse to frighten away the demon. Other cultures also used legends to explain what was happening in the sky.

The next total eclipse is projected to occur in August of 2008, but there are partial eclipses that occur from time to time. Check out the NASA web site for the next one visible in your area of the world.

### Pinhole Viewer

It is very important NEVER to look directly at the sun during any solar eclipse, and telescopes and binoculars should only be used with proper filters. The safest way to view a solar eclipse is with a pinhole viewer. Here's how to make your own.

**You Need**

- Paper punch (¼-inch size)
- 2 sheets of white cardboard

Punch a hole in the middle of the first sheet of cardboard. Stand with your back to the sun. Hold the cardboard with the hole in it so that the sun comes through the hole. Hold the other piece of cardboard parallel to the first about a foot away. The farther away the piece of cardboard is, the larger the image will appear. You should see the image of the eclipse on the second piece of cardboard. Experiment with moving the two sheets closer and farther away to get a clear image.

## Solar Power

The sun powers our planet in many ways. Some are direct and others indirect. For instance, the sun "feeds" plants through the process of *photosynthesis* while indirectly supplying us with power. Ancient plants that processed the sun's energy by photosynthesis are now the coal, oil, and peat we use as fossil fuel. *Solar panels*, a direct form of sun power, energize everything from calculators to houses. And the sun also makes the wind blow, energy which we channel with windmills and wind turbines. Let's investigate some of the ways to use the sun's energy.

## Harness the Sun by Day, Read at Night

You have probably seen square, flat, solar cells on calculators or buildings. These cells or panels work to harness the light from the sun and convert it to electricity. The scientific term for this type of solar energy is called *photovoltaic energy*. The cells are known as *photovoltaic cells* (PVs) or solar cells.

Sunlight is made up of particles of solar energy called *photons*. When the photons hit a solar cell, they are absorbed or reflected, or they can pass right through the cell, depending upon the amount of energy they contain. Only the absorbed photons will provide energy to generate electricity.

There are a couple of drawbacks to solar energy. Sunlight is not reliable because not all days are sunny, and the area that's required to collect the light to make it worthwhile is very large.

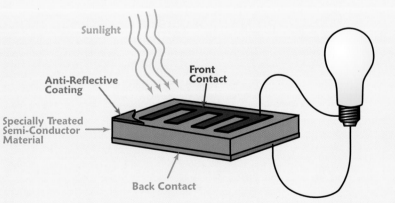

Sunlight

Anti-Reflective
Coating

Front
Contact

Specially Treated
Semi-Conductor
Material

Back Contact

## A Pinwheel

The sun warms the Earth, but the Earth isn't warmed evenly. It is warmer at the equator (the imaginary line that circles the Earth) than at the North and South Poles, because the equator receives roughly the same amount of sunlight all year. When the air is warmed at the equator, it rises into the atmosphere and flows toward the poles. The cold air from the poles flows to take its place. This movement creates wind. A windmill or wind turbine to generate wind power can harness the wind. It is an inexpensive and clean alternative power source. A pinwheel is a mini-windmill. Here's how to make your own.

**You Need**

- Square sheet of paper (8 x 8 inches)
- Ruler
- Pencil with eraser
- Scissors
- Pin

Lay the sheet of paper on the table and, with the ruler, draw a diagonal line from each corner to the opposite corner. With the tip of the pencil, punch a hole in the middle of the square, where the two lines intersect. Cut along each line until you reach about one inch from the center. Poke a small hole in the left-hand corner of each of the four flaps. Keep in mind that no two holes should be next to each other. Hold one of the flaps at the corner with the hole and curve it to the center hole. Poke the pin through it to hold it in place. Repeat with each of the four flaps until the pin is holding all of the flaps together. Gently pick up the pinwheel and pin it to the side of the eraser on the pencil. In order to see your pinwheel spin, turn it to face the wind. When the wind hits the center of the pinwheel, it will rotate just like a windmill.

# Try This ⬇

## Solar-Powered S'more Snack

The next time you go camping or are planning a picnic, you can cook without a campfire with this simple solar-powered can cooker. Here's a recipe to make a favorite snack: S'mores.

**You Need**

- Pringles can or similar snack can
- Scissors
- Metal skewer
- Marshmallows
- Graham crackers
- Chocolate bar

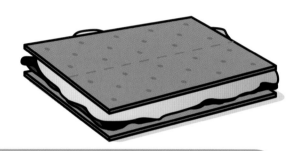

Clean out the inside of the snack can. Ask a grownup to cut a lengthwise slit in the can, leaving about an inch at each end. Cut another slit, about an inch long, across each end of the slit. Carefully pull back the sides of the slit exposing the foil-lined inside of the can. The foil inside is perfect for reflecting the warm rays of the sun. Ask a grownup to help you poke the skewer through the can. Poke one side of the skewer through the can and place a couple of marshmallows on it. Poke the other side through so that it rests in the can. The skewer acts like a spit in your mini can-oven. Place your cooker in direct sunlight off the ground on a table or a rock. Make sure the sun is shining on your marshmallows. Turn the skewer every so often and watch your marshmallows. When your marshmallows are soft, sandwich them between the graham crackers and a piece of chocolate. Try your cooker on another day with a hot dog.

## Vitamins from the Sun

We've seen the energy that the sun can generate, but how does the sun power us? When the sun's ultraviolet light shines on us, our body produces *vitamin D* in our skin. Vitamin D helps our bodies absorb calcium and keep our bones strong, but scientists also believe that it plays an even bigger role. It is now thought that a lack of vitamin D can lead to increased cancer risks. There is a fine balance between getting enough vitamin D from sunshine and risking damage to our skin with the ultraviolet rays. A sunscreen is still recommended, but it's crucial to also have some sun exposure without a sunscreen.

*The largest solar flare ever recorded, 4:51 PM EDT, Monday, April 2, 2001*

## Solar Flares

During the fall of 2003 scientists witnessed some of the greatest *solar flares* ever recorded. A solar flare is a sudden explosion of the sun's atmosphere, called *corona*. During a solar flare, the amount of energy released within the span of just a few minutes could be equal to billions of atomic bombs. Flares often occur near *sunspots* which is a region on the surface of the sun with lower temperature but with intense magnetic activity.

These flares, although 150 million kilometers away from us, still impact our planet. During one recent solar flare, communication satellites in space—that help us talk over long distances without wires—were temporarily shut down; airlines were routed away from high altitudes for fear they would encounter communication problems; and 50,000 people in southern Sweden briefly lost power.

## Solar Power

Could you believe there could be any connection between solar flares and violins? Could solar flares cause whales to beach themselves? Scientists are examining the pattern of solar flares and seeing some of these connections.

Between 1645 and 1715, there was a reduction in solar flares and a dip in temperatures. This cold spell in Europe may have slowed tree growth which created the ideal wood for violin makers, such as the famed Antonio Stradivari, whose violins sell for millions of dollars.

The cycle of higher solar flare activity runs from eight to seventeen years, with eleven being the average. That means that every eleven years or so the sun goes through a period of more frequent solar flares. Scientists have looked at the sightings of beached sperm whales between the years of 1712 and 2003 and have discovered more whale beachings during the periods of greater sun activity. German scientists have theorized that the increased flares throw off the whale's inner compass and cause them to veer off their normal migration paths.

*Northern lights as seen from NASA's satellite*

## Aurora Borealis

When solar flares hit Earth's upper atmosphere, they give off bursts of X-rays and charged particles and can spawn an aurora, also known as the northern lights. The name *aurora borealis* comes from the Latin words for "red dawn of the north" and was coined by the Italian scientist Galileo Galilei (1564-1642). Galileo lived on a latitude where the northern lights were mostly red in color. In Norway, where the lights are often seen, they are called *Nordlys* or *Polarlys*. Check out Nordlys at www.northern-lights.no/ for a space weather forecast and more information about northern lights.

*Northern lights in the winter sky*

## Think about It!

Put your scientist's hat on. Scientists are constantly asking questions. If you were a scientist, what would you be interested in investigating along with the cycles of solar flares? Could there be a correlation between solar flare activity and storms or other animal activity? Or perhaps there is a correlation between flares and the activity of humans? Wouldn't it be interesting to study the flares for the last 500 years and the events that happened in our history?

## Starry Night

Our sun is not the only shining star in our sky. We see a whole sky full of stars each night. Now that we have explored our very own star, let's travel farther away and begin our deep sky exploration of the rest of the stars shining down on us.

# Star Lights

Have you ever looked up at night and spied the first star? Each one of the twinkling white lights you see in the night sky is a giant spinning ball of hot gas, just like our sun. Each is a massive power plant, producing great amounts of energy in the form of light and heat. Some are smaller than our sun and others are much larger. It's hard to tell the size when we look at them; but if we could see their colors, we would be able to tell how big and how hot they are. Although they all look white to us, they are really different colors.

Star light, star bright,
First star I see tonight,
I wish I may, I wish I might,
Have the wish I wish tonight.

## Colorful Stars

What we now know is that stars, like metal, change color when they are heated. If you heat metal, it will become red-hot. With more heat, it will turn orange, then yellow, and finally white-hot. This is similar to the relation of heat and color in stars. Stars burn hydrogen. The more hydrogen they burn, the hotter they are and their color changes. There are small red stars, medium yellow stars, large white stars, and giant blue stars. Our sun is a yellow star. It is not as hot as a large white star, but it is hotter than a small red star. Giant blue stars burn more hydrogen than any other star and are, therefore, the hottest.

### So What's Hydrogen?

Hydrogen is a gas that is the lightest of all gases and the most abundant element in the universe.

# Face of SPACE

## Annie Jump Canon

On December 11, 1863, a little girl was born in Dover, Delaware, who would grow up to become an astronomical spectroscopist and spend much of her life deciphering the colors of the stars. Her name was Annie Jump Cannon. Annie said, "Classifying the stars has helped materially in all studies of the structure of the universe."

## So What's a Spectroscopist?

A *spectroscopist* is a person who investigates and measures spectra, or energy, coming from a source in the universe.

*An example of one type of spectroscope*

# Galaxies

Put about 10 billion stars together and you have a galaxy. There are over 100 billion galaxies in the universe. We can see three galaxies from Earth without using a telescope: the Magellanic Clouds, which are actually two galaxies named after the Portuguese explorer Ferdinand Magellen, and the Andromeda galaxy, which is about 2.2 million light-years away from Earth. (That's about the same as 13,200,000,000,000,000,000 miles from New York.) We can also see part of our own galaxy, the Milky Way. Light from our Milky Way takes 25,000 years to reach us!

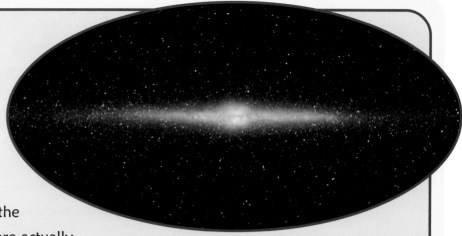

*An x-ray mosaic of the Milky Way, © by Ned Wright*

Galaxies come in many different shapes. There are elliptical galaxies that are giant oval balls of stars. There are also spiral galaxies, like the Milky Way and Andromeda, which look like swirly lollipops. There are galaxies that have almost no shape at all. Sometimes galaxies collide and merge to form an even bigger galaxy.

## Think about It!

If you could see the Milky Way from the side, it would look like a flat plate with a bulge in the middle. It takes 225 million years for the Milky Way to spin completely around. It has over 100 billion stars and, even with that large number, is not the biggest galaxy in the universe.

## So What's a Galaxy?

A *galaxy* is a collection of stars, gas, and dust, and the word *galaxy* comes from the Greek word *gala*, meaning milk.

I'd like some gala and cookies.

# Face of SPACE

## Heidi Jo Newberg

Heidi Jo Newberg wanted to be a teacher when she was young. Today she's a physicist and astronomer at Rensselaer Polytechnic Institute (RPI) in Troy, New York, and the mother of four children. She teaches physics and astronomy courses and researches galaxies. Her children are proud to have a scientist for a mom.

Heidi always liked math and science. She earned a degree in physics from RPI and later went to the University of California at Berkeley for her graduate studies. She found that she always asked why things were the way they were. Now she is searching for the origin of galaxies, one of the biggest questions facing astronomers.

You might think that astronomers spend their time looking through telescopes; but in fact, most astronomers spend much of their time analyzing the data that is collected from the large mountain-top telescopes all over the world. Digital cameras take images through the telescopes and the data is fed into computers. Heidi spent time as a student collecting data; now she digs through the data others collect and comes up with interesting ways to look at it.

Heidi believes that good scientists are also creative people. She played the French horn when she was young and still enjoys painting and beading. Imagination helps a scientist look at things differently.

### Think about It!

It's difficult to imagine so many stars and so many galaxies in the sky. Here's a way to think about galaxies that might help. Take out a jar of sugar. Imagine that each grain of sugar is a star. Spoon a tablespoon of sugar onto a table. Then add another tablespoon farther away on the table. Add one more. The galaxies are similarly positioned in deep sky. In between are vast areas of dark space with other floating bodies, like asteroids.

## Constellations

If the night is clear and there aren't a lot of lights from buildings or roads nearby, it's fun to gaze up at the sky and see if you can connect the stars that dot the sky. People have been doing just that for thousands of years. Those pictures they create from connecting the stars are known as *constellations*. People usually saw images of things that interested them and fit into their lives. For example, if people spent a good deal of time hunting, they might see wild animals and hunters in the stars, like the constellation Ursa Major or the Great Bear. Another is the archer Orion. Many of the constellations were named after Greek mythological characters.

## Try This ↓

### Connect the Stars

What do you think you would see in the stars if you didn't know any of the constellations and you just had a sky full of stars to look at? How would you connect the dots? Let's see.

**You Need**

- A star chart without any names (look in the Resources section for info on star charts)
- A highlighter

Take a look at the star chart in front of you. Forget about any of the constellation shapes you have learned and pretend you are looking at the sky for the first time. How would you connect the stars to make pictures? Use your highlighter to trace the shape in your stars. Connect the stars like you would play connect the dots.

That's a lot of dots!

## The Great Bear: An Iroquois Legend of Ursa Major

In the cold winter of long, long ago, a big bear attacked and devoured the wild game the Iroquois hunted for food. The hunters were unable to catch the bear. As soon as they got close enough to shoot an arrow, the bear would vanish.

One night three brothers dreamed they found the bear. They took this as a sign and set out the next morning with their dog to search for the bear. Often they saw him, but as they got closer, the bear would vanish. They trailed the bear day and night. Eventually they arrived at the edge of the world where it touches the northern sky. Through the icy

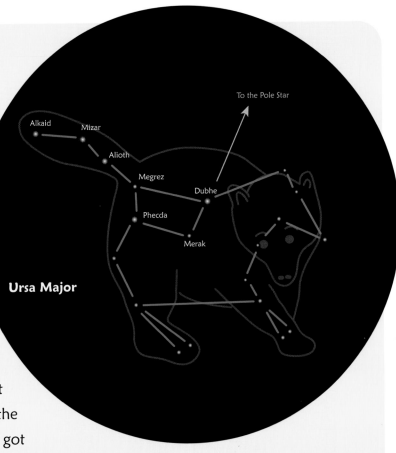

**Ursa Major**

mists and white clouds, they saw the bear running through the snow.

They climbed higher on the paths and into the sky. They finally found the bear asleep in a cave. The bear woke up just as the hunters threw a net over it. The great bear grabbed the net, gathered up the hunters, and flung them into the sky.

### A Look Back

The story of the bear among the stars was not unique to the Iroquois. Many early people told a story of the Great Bear, including the Greeks, Hebrews, and tribes in Siberia. The fact that people in Eurasia and North America told similar stories of the bear and the dipper points to the early hunters and gatherers who migrated to North America across a land bridge that stretched across the Bering Strait. These early people passed down their stories in the New World, which most likely included the stories of the stars.

If you look up you will see the hunters. They are the three stars in the handle of the constellation the Big Dipper, part of the constellation Ursa Major. The four stars that make up the bowl of the dipper create the constellation of the Great Bear.

## Big Dipper Puzzle

Find a picture of the Big Dipper constellation and make this puzzle
to carry around with you.

**You Need**

- Two-part metal canning jar lid
- Plastic sheet (like from the top of a greeting card box)
- Scissors
- Tape
- Cardboard
- String
- White glue
- Pellets (BBs or beads)
- Pen

Remove the inner
portion of the metal lid.
Place the lid on the plastic
and trace around it. Cut out
the circle from the plastic. Tape
the plastic inside the metal lid. Cut out
the same size circle from the cardboard. Take the string and
measure the circumference of the circle. Ask a grownup to help you
cut a strip of cardboard about a half-inch wide and the length of the
string (to fit around the cardboard circle). Tape the ends of the strip
together. Glue the cardboard band around the circle and hold it until
it sticks. On the cardboard, use the pen to place dots where the stars
are located in the Big Dipper constellation. Poke each dot with a
hole that is slightly smaller than the pellet. Finish your puzzle by
adding the pellets and the metal lid. See if you can move the dish to
get the pellets in each of the star locations. Try creating another
puzzle with a different constellation.

# The Drinking Gourd

People describe constellations with different names. The slaves in early America called the constellation we call the Big Dipper, the Drinking Gourd. By drying out a gourd and cutting it open, the slaves could make a cup with a handle, like a dipper, to scoop out drinking water from a bucket. To them, the constellation of the Big Dipper was shaped like their drinking gourd. It also had another meaning to them.

They knew that if they followed the constellation of the Drinking Gourd north, they would eventually find their freedom through the Underground Railroad. They sang a song to tell other slaves about the path to freedom.

I thought I heard the angels say
Follow the Drinking Gourd.
The stars in the heavens gonna
   show you the way.
Follow the Drinking Gourd.

Here's another translation of a stanza of the song.

When the sun comes back and
   the first quail calls,
Follow the Drinking Gourd.
For the old man is waiting for
   to carry you to freedom,
If you follow the Drinking Gourd.

The initial line of this stanza "When the sun comes back and the first quail calls," tells us that the slaves knew how to use the sun to track time. In the winter and spring, the sun's angle above the horizon gets higher each day at noon until the beginning of summer. In summer and fall the sun gets lower each day. The song line told the slaves to leave in the winter when the sunlight grows each day.

Each line of the song gave the slaves their specific instructions on the path they would need to follow to reach freedom. You can learn more about the Underground Railroad in the Resources section.

Little Dipper

North Star

Big Dipper
(The Gourd)

Find the constellation Ursa Minor on a star chart. It looks very much like the Big Dipper but smaller, and the handle turns in the opposite direction. The last star in the handle of Ursa Minor, or the Little Dipper, is the star Polaris, also called the *North Star.*

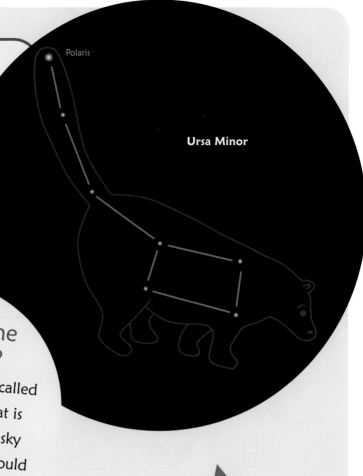

Polaris

**Ursa Minor**

### So What's the North Star?

The *North Star* is also called *Polaris.* It is a star that is constant in the night sky and by which sailors could navigate.

## Star Navigation

With only the legends of the sea, wind, and stars, ancient people set out in their canoes and ships for new lands. The sailors would search the skies for the North Star. The North Star never seemed to move. It is the star that the Earth's axis, the imaginary straight line that runs through the center of the planet, points toward in the Northern sky. When sailors located the North Star, they could find their latitude and chart their course.

In the days of Christopher Columbus's travels, it was usually impossible to also measure longitude, the imaginary lines that stretch from North Pole to South Pole on the Earth. Latitude, the imaginary lines that run north and south of the equator, was easily obtained by measuring the star and the angle between the star and an overhead point, called the *zenith.* This process was known as *celestial navigation.*

### So What's a Zenith?

The *zenith* is the highest point reached by an object.

## A Native American Legend of the North Star

Na-Gah, was a brave son who wanted to impress his father, so he set out to climb the tallest cliff he could find. He climbed and climbed until he reached the top of a very high mountain. He was so high that he could look down on all the other mountains around him. When his father came searching for him, he found his son high on the mountain with no way to climb down. The father was proud of his brave son and did not want him to suffer. He turned Na-Gah into a star that everyone and every living thing could see and honor. He became the North Star.

## So What's Precession?

*Precession* is the change in a rotating body's orbit as it responds to gravitational pull.

## The Pole Stars

The North Star, or Pole Star that exists today, named Polaris, wasn't always the North Star. Over thousands of years, our Earth shifted a little on its axis, and so in the history of our planet there have been other stars that pointed north. These include the stars, Alderamin, Vega, and Thuban. At times in our planet's history, there was no star exactly to the north. Scientists call the shifting of the stars the process of precession.

## A Star Theater

Here's a way to look at the stars on the next cloudy night. Bring them indoors, pull out a blanket, and have your own indoor star party.

**You Need**

- Scissors
- Cardboard quart milk carton
- Marker
- Thumbtack
- Flashlight

Ask a grownup to cut off the top of the milk carton. Use the marker to draw a constellation on the bottom of the milk carton. Place a dot where each star is located. Ask a grownup to help you pierce holes in the bottom with the tack where each star is found. Place the flashlight inside the box and turn it on in a dark room. Point the light to the ceiling to create your constellation.

# The Birth of a Star

A star may seem to be in the sky forever, but actually stars have a beginning and an end. They are "born." At first gravity pulls gas and dust into huge clumps inside a *nebula* such as the Orion Nebula. The nebulae are sometimes called *stellar nurseries* and pictures taken of them with the Hubble telescope are spectacular. The photographs that are taken usually show the nebula with a red hue, but that's not always the case. In the Rosette Nebula, found in the constellation Monoceros, sulfur emissions glow red, hydrogen emissions glow blue, and oxygen emissions glow green. The resulting nebula image looks more like an abstract painting than the night sky.

Eventually the clumps inside the nebula shrink into balls, which get smaller and hotter. The results are new stars. The center of a new star becomes hot enough for the gas to make energy and shine steadily.

So What's a Nebula?
A *nebula* is a cloud of gas and dust in outer space but visible in the night sky.

*The Rosette Nebula, 3,000 light years away from Earth, © by NOAO*

# The Death of a Star

Stars also have an end. They die in several ways. A star will someday reach a point when it has burned up most of its gases in the center. It will swell up like an inflated beach ball until it becomes so large that gravity forces it to collapse in a matter of seconds. It then becomes a *white dwarf.* Our sun will someday become a white dwarf when it runs out of helium to burn. White dwarfs are not really stars because they do not generate energy by fusing lighter elements into heavier elements.

## So What's a Pulsar?

A *pulsar* is a star that emits pulses of radio waves and other electromagnetic radiation.

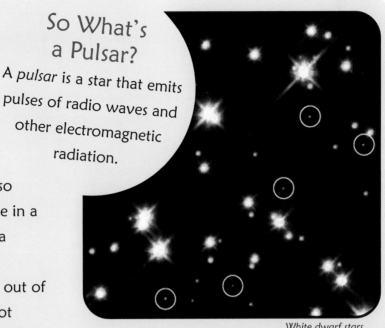

*White dwarf stars*

## So What's a Nova?

A star that suddenly gets brighter and then, over a few months, retreats to its original brightness is called a *nova.*

They are very hot, though, and still look like a star because they shine light as they cool. When a white dwarf finally cools, all that remains is black rock, called a *black dwarf.*

Heavier stars, which contain a greater amount of heavier elements, will end their lives, instead, by exploding as type II *supernovae.* These supernovae can leave behind a neutron star or *pulsar* at their centers. It is believed that heavier stars can leave a black hole behind, where gravity is so strong light cannot escape.

Not all stars inflate and then collapse at their end. Often a star and a white dwarf are orbiting one another around a common center of mass, like a planet or other body. When the star expands, for instance, as it evolves to be a giant, it transfers matter to the white dwarf. The matter could cause a small nuclear explosion (nova) or cause the star to blow apart entirely (supernova type Ia). Sometimes the star is not completely destroyed. The gas and dust particles that made up the star become part of the nebula once more.

## So What's a Supernova?

A star that suddenly gets much brighter because of an explosion in which it loses most of its mass is called a *supernova.*

## Light Pollution

Can there ever be too much light in the sky? Apparently yes. Sometimes there is so much light from buildings and streets that the light can prevent you from seeing the stars at night. Too much light is known as *light pollution*.

**Think about It!**

You can join forces with the International Dark-Sky Association to "preserve and protect the nighttime environment and our heritage of dark skies through quality outdoor lighting." The Association's goal is to stop the effects of light pollution on dark skies, raise awareness about light pollution and its solutions, and educate everyone about the value of quality outdoor lighting. Here's how you can help.

• Replace the high wattage light bulbs outside your house with low wattage ones to reduce stray light.

• Celebrate National Dark-Sky Week. Jennifer Barlow founded this event in 2003 when she became concerned about light pollution. National Dark-Sky Week occurs on the week of the new moon in April since a full moon increases the light pollution. This is the perfect time to host a star party.

• Find out if there is a lighting code in your community. Someone in your town hall or village office should be able to answer your question. Bring a grownup along with you. If not, encourage the officials to develop a code.

• If your community abides by certain lighting codes, it might qualify to be an International Dark-Sky Community. Check out the Association's web site to nominate your community: www.darksky.org.

# Try This ↓

## Have a Super Star Party

Have you ever been to a star party? This isn't the Hollywood kind of star party. No red carpets here, just a clear night, a telescope, and some friends. Well, maybe a little more. Here's how to plan your own star party for National Astronomy Day or any clear night.

### What You Need

- Telescope
- Blanket and chairs
- Star chart
- Red light flashlight
- Binoculars
- Friends
- Picnic snacks

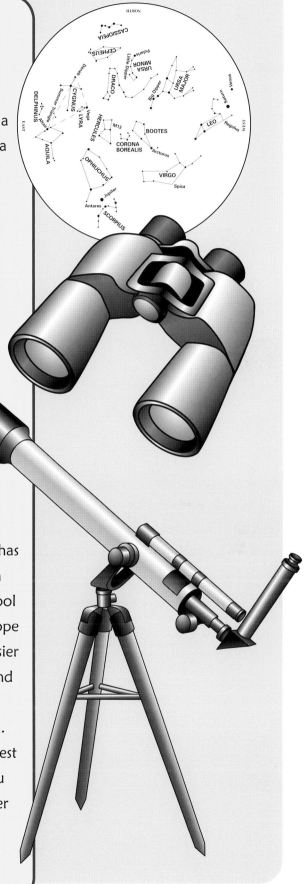

Get plenty of sleep the night before your star party or take a nap during the day because you will be up very late at night watching the stars. Locate a dark-sky area. Many of us live in light-polluted areas that don't enable us to view the night sky easily. Find a place that has little, if any, artificial light at night. Dress for the night in layers of clothing. Even in the summer it can get very cool when the sun goes down. It's best to set up your telescope at dusk. You can adjust it during the evening, but it's easier to position it in the light. Spread your blanket nearby and open up your chairs. When it gets dark, check your star chart with your red flashlight and begin your star search.

Can you find the North Star, Polaris? It's the brightest and last star in the handle of the Little Dipper. Once you have located Polaris, you will be able to find many other stars on your chart. Make sure everyone gets to peek through the telescope or the binoculars. While waiting your turn, munch on the snacks you brought along.

# Try This ↓

## Star Chart

A *star chart* is like a road map to the stars, but instead of looking down, you read a star chart looking up. Hold the star chart above your head. Use a compass to help you face south. Position the north horizon on the chart behind you and the south horizon in front of you. Keep in mind that the sky above you is much larger than your chart and there are many more stars in the sky. Use a red flashlight to help you read your chart in the dark. It will help preserve your night vision. If you move, remember to also move your star chart.

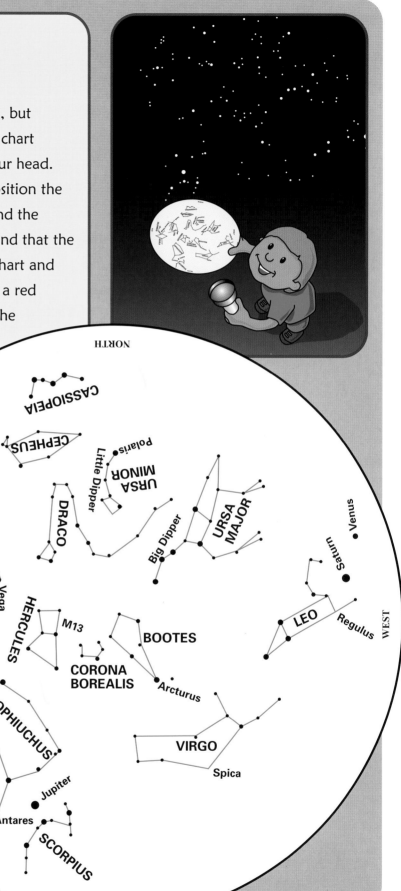

## So What's a Constellation?

A *constellation* is a group of stars that is said to resemble and named after an animal, an inanimate object, or a mythological character.

## Pleiades Ladies

The Pleiades cluster of stars, known, as the "Seven Sisters" is located in the constellation Taurus. Scientists claim the cluster of hot, bluish white stars is no more than 50 million years old, young for a star cluster. The Pleiades have been recognized since very early times and are mentioned in the Bible and Homer's *Odyssey*. On a clear night, you can easily make out the seven brightest stars in the cluster. See if you can see any more with binoculars. The cluster is actually home to around 400 stars.

*The Pleiades*, © by ROE/AAO

## Make It!

### A Star Chart

Once you are able to read a star chart and locate the stars on a clear night, you can try your hand at making your own star chart. Here's how.

**You Need**

- Paper
- Colored pencils

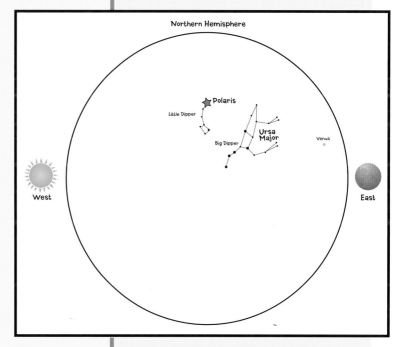

Draw a large circle on your paper. On the outside of the top of the circle write Northern Hemisphere. Draw a picture of the sun setting in the west horizon. Draw a picture of the moon rising in the east, opposite the sun. Draw Polaris where it would appear. Draw one more constellation on your chart.

# The Stars:
## Our Magic Eight Ball

Many people rely on the stars to tell them what their day will be like or their month, week, or year. They look to the stars to tell them if they will get along with their spouse or friends. And they look at profiles of themselves written in the stars. This is nothing new. Many scientists believe that the signs of the *zodiac* began close to 4,000 years ago with the Babylonians in the Middle East.

But what exactly are the zodiac symbols and how do they tell us our future? As you know, the sun, moon, and planets move in a circle around the sky. All of these objects pass through the same constellations as they make their circle. The ancient people looked at this circle and divided it into twelve constellations.

The sun took one month to travel through each one. These people looked at the constellations and saw many shapes of animals and, therefore, named this the zodiac, meaning "circle of animals." This zodiac was passed on to the ancient Greeks, Egyptians, and the Chinese. The Japanese zodiac features animals such as the rat, tiger, and monkey.

The study of the zodiac is known as *astrology.* It is not astronomy. According to NASA there were originally thirteen symbols and not twelve. Because Earth's axis has shifted, the zodiac signs are no longer accurate. Taking this into account, someone born today under the sign Cancer, might actually be born under the constellation Gemini. You should not take your zodiac predictions seriously, but they can be fun to read.

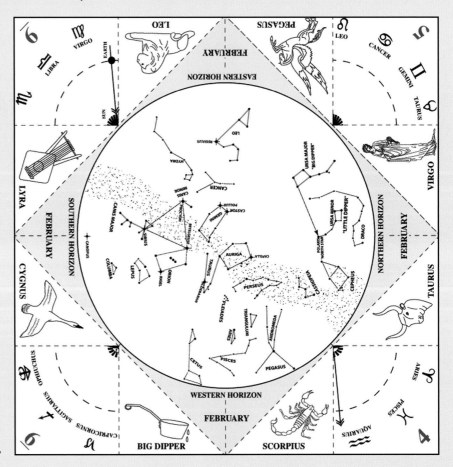

## Make It!

### Starry, Starry Night

Perhaps one of the most well-known paintings of the nighttime sky was painted by Vincent Van Gogh and is titled *The Starry Night*. It shows the nighttime sky full of movement. Most people find it a very emotional painting. Look for a copy of the painting *The Starry Night* on the Internet (try: http://artchive.com/artchive/V/van_gogh/starry_night.jpg.html) and see what you think. Then paint your own starry night.

**You Need**

- White paper
- Pencil
- Tempera paints
- White painting paper
- Paintbrushes
- Water
- Sponges

The Starry Night *by Vincent Van Gogh*

Look at how Van Gogh painted his night sky. Look in the Resources section for more paintings that depict the night sky. Van Gogh uses swirls and brush strokes to create the look of wind in his painting. Think about what you want to draw and how you can capture your feeling of the starry night. Use the plain white paper to try out some of your ideas. Sketch out your design with the pencil. When you are ready, use the tempera paint on the white painting paper to create your starry night painting. Remember to wash out your brush and use a separate piece of paper to mix your colors. Experiment with the sponges to get other shapes in your painting.

### Moving on to the Moon

Moving a little closer to home, we cannot forget to explore the centerpiece of our night sky: the moon. It follows us on our evening walks. It glows like a bright ball in the night sky. We mark our days by it. We track our moods by it. We've even placed a human foot on it. Let's start our own lunar expedition now. Just turn the page.

Star Lights **77**

# Marvelous Moons

> **"That's one small step for a man, one giant leap for mankind."—Neil Armstrong**

On July 20, 1969, history was made. For the first time in the history of humankind, humans left our planet and placed a foot on another celestial body in our universe—the moon. Astronaut Neil Armstrong stepped from the lunar module, the Eagle, six hours after landing and placed his foot on the moon's rocky surface. Astronaut Buzz Aldrin joined him shortly after.

For the first time, the men looked up into the sky above them and, instead of seeing the moon or sun, they saw Earth. Neil Armstrong later said, "It suddenly struck me that that tiny pea, pretty and blue, was Earth. I put up my thumb and shut one eye, and my thumb blotted out the planet Earth. I didn't feel like a giant. I felt very, very small."

How amazing that view must have been. Not many will ever share that experience, but we're leaping ahead. Let's step back a little and discover the moons in our solar system from here on Earth.

## Our Tidal Atmosphere

If the moon influences the ocean tides, do you think it could also influence our atmosphere? It actually does have some influence. The air in our atmosphere flows like the water in our oceans but unlike the ocean tides, the sun rather than the moon has the greater influence on the atmospheric tides.

## Our Moon

Look up at the night sky and what do you see? As long as man has lived on Earth, he has gazed up at the heavens and seen a glowing round ball in the night sky we call the *moon*. Prehistoric man looked up at night and saw it. The Native Americans long ago saw the same moon. The ancient Greeks saw the moon and called it *Selene*. The ancient Romans saw the moon and called it *Luna*. Even with other names, it is the same moon that we still see.

## Glowing Light

Does the moon glow? It looks like it does. On a night when the moon is a full round circle, the Earth is lit up; but the moon doesn't really emit the glowing light itself, as the sun does. The moon reflects the light of the sun; it does not shine on its own.

*Buzz Aldrin plants the U.S. flag on the moon July 20, 1969.*

## Moovin' Moon

The moon is not always a large round ball shining in the night sky. Sometimes it looks like it was cut in half, and at other times during the month it looks as if it's only a sliver. The moon does not really change shape during the month. The moon cycles around our planet, and because of this we cannot always see the whole moon. It moves its width every hour.

| 1 | 2 | 3 | 4 | 5 | 6 | 7 | 8 | 1 |

## Think about It!

The changing positions of the moon make up the lunar cycle. The first phase of the moon is known as the new moon. From the new moon to the full moon the moon looks like it is growing bigger. We call this period *waxing*. The moon enters the waxing crescent moon phase, then the quarter moon, and finally the almost-full gibbous moon before it is completely full. After the full moon, night after night the moon looks like it is getting smaller and is known as *waning*. It goes through the same phases as it moves toward the next new moon.

## So What's a Lunar Cycle?

The *lunar cycle* is the one complete orbit of the moon around the Earth and characterized by the different phases.

## Experiment with the Moon

Can you see the moon from your house at night? If you can, here's a way to check out the moon's phases right from your own window.

**You Need**

- Clock
- Tape
- Tracing paper
- Pencil

Search your house for a window that has a view of the moon. Check the time that you can see the moon from that window. Tape the sheet of tracing paper to the window so that it covers the entire moon. Use the pencil to trace the shape of the moon on your paper. Look at the moon the next night at the same time and trace the moon's image on the same paper. Is the moon the same shape? How has it changed? Try it again the next night. Has the moon's shape changed again? Has it moved in the sky? How do your pictures compare to the pictures of the lunar phases?

## Roman Calendar

In ancient Rome, the months were as long as a lunar cycle. Each of the months was divided into three sections that ended on the day of one of the first three moon phases: new, first quarter, or full. *Calends*, from the Latin word *calare* meaning to announce or call out, was the name for the first day of each month. Our word calendar was derived from this custom.

## Have You Heard of a Blue Moon?

Have you ever heard anyone say that something happens "once in a blue moon" and wondered what he or she meant? A *blue moon* is not really blue at all, it looks the same as any other full moon. But it's different because it's the second full moon in the same month or the third full moon in a season that has four. Composers Rodgers and Hart wrote a popular song in 1934, called "Blue Moon." Watch the movie *Grease* and you'll hear it!

## Crazy Night of the Full Moon

Do werewolves really come out at night when there is a full moon? Are there really more crimes, births, and accidents? In 1996, Ivan Kelly, James Rotton, and Roger Culver examined over 100 studies on the effects of the moon and came to the conclusion that these studies did not determine the correlation between the full moon and crimes, birthrates, and the craziness of behavior that is often blamed on the full moon or other lunar phases.

Many myths associated with full moons are rooted in ancient folklore and continued by our society. And of course, werewolves are not real! Go outside during the next full-moon night and take a walk. It's the perfect time for a firefly hunt, an owl prowl, or a stargazing party.

## The Wonderful World of Tides

If you have ever visited the ocean, you will know that there are times when the water is farther up the beach than at other times. This occurs because of the tides. There are low tides and high tides. The gravitational pull of the moon and the sun produce two tidal bulges on opposite sides of the Earth. The moon, however, because it is much closer to the Earth, has much more influence on the tides than the sun.

When the moon orbits Earth, the water on the planet bulges and moves with it. If you have experienced a new or full moon on a visit to the ocean, you have experienced what is called a *spring tide*. A spring tide is a particularly large tide. A *neap tide*, which is weaker, occurs during a first quarter or last quarter moon.

So What's a Tide?
The *tides* are the alternate rising and falling of the sea due to the gravitational pull of the sun and moon.

*A full moon over the ocean's edge*

## Make It!

### Moon Cakes

Follow this recipe for yummy moon cakes.

**You Need**
- Bowl
- ¼ cup sugar
- 2 egg yolks
- ½ cup salted butter, softened
- Spoon
- 1 cup flour
- Plastic wrap
- Teaspoon
- Cookie sheet
- 1 cup red bean paste
  (jam can be substituted)
- Pastry brush

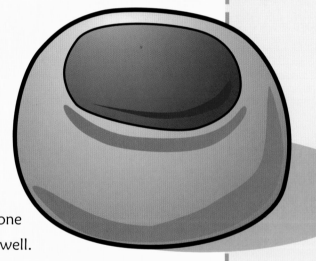

Preheat the oven to 375°F.
In the bowl, combine sugar, one
egg yolk, and butter and stir well.
Add the flour. Use your hands to form the
mixture into a large ball of dough and wrap it in plastic
wrap. Refrigerate the dough for about thirty minutes.
Unwrap the dough and shape it into about twenty-four
balls. Make a hole in each ball with your finger and add
one-half teaspoon red bean paste or jam. Place on a cookie
sheet. Beat the other egg yolk and brush it over the top of
each moon cake. Bake moon cakes for about twenty
minutes or until the edges are brown.

### Chinese Moon Festival

When the moon is full in the autumn, the Chinese celebrate the Harvest Moon Festival. This celebration dates back to the Tang Dynasty in AD 618. The Chinese thank the moon goddess for the good harvest and ask for a good harvest again next year. Chinese families celebrate with reunions, moon-watching events, moon poems, and sweet moon cakes.

## Try This ↓

Sometimes Chinese families have a ceremony to capture the moon. You can catch the moon's reflection, too, in a bowl of water just like they do in China! Write a moon poem to go with your celebration and invite your friends to do the same. Read the poems together under the full moon. Don't forget to make a wish. The festival moon is considered lucky.

## So What's a Dynasty?

The hereditary rulers of China are called a *dynasty*.

## Think about It!

Ancient people recorded the moon's cycle by giving each a name that usually pertained to the harvests or other important events in their lives. For example, can you guess which month would have a Strawberry Moon? If you guessed the month of June, the time when strawberries become ripe in the fields, you would be correct. Snow Moons fell during the winter months.

## Try This ↓

Here are some more moons of the month. Take a look and then try coming up with your own moon names.

| Full Wolf Moon | January |
| Full Snow Moon | February |
| Full Sap Moon | March |
| Full Egg Moon | April |
| Full Blossom Moon | May |
| Full Strawberry Moon | June |
| Full Thunder Moon | July |
| Full Green Corn Moon | August |
| Full Grain Moon | September |
| Full Hunter's Moon | October |
| Full Beaver Moon | November |
| Full Oak Moon | December |

## The Moon's Surface

When astronauts first stepped on the moon's surface, they found it dusty and rocky and filled with craters, both large and small. There were also cracks in the surface as well as some smooth areas. When you look at the moon, you will notice that parts of the moon look darker and some look lighter. Take a look at the moon with binoculars and you will be able to see the characteristics of both of these regions. The dark regions of the moon, known as *maria* after the Latin word for seas, are smooth, low-lying plains with few craters. The lighter regions are hillier with many craters and are covered with a light colored rock called *anorthosite*. You may be able to see a moon rock in a museum.

## Think about It!

It might look like there's a face in the moon. Legend says that it's the man in the moon, and there are many stories about this fellow. Early Christian peasants told their children that the man in the moon was a man who refused to admit Jesus to the warmth of his hearth and was banished to the moon. The Japanese people don't talk about a "man in the moon;" they talk about a rabbit in the moon. What do you see?

## Mapping the Moon

Many craters of the moon have been identified and named. Would you guess that Julius Caesar, Archimedes, Beer, Newton, and Billy are the names of craters? The mapping of the moon is divided into quadrants. The First Quadrant, or northeast, is where the Apollo 11 and Apollo 17 astronauts landed. Among the craters there are also mountain peaks over 13,000 feet (4,000 m) high. The other quadrants have mountains, valleys, and craters also that are mapped and named. You can see many craters with a good telescope and compare your findings with moon maps.

## Moon Craters

Dig in and get your hands dirty creating these moon craters. When you finish, visit the Resources section for a great web site with photos of the actual moon surface. How does yours compare?

**You Need**

- Newspaper
- A circle cut out of poster board
- 6 cups flour
- ½ cup water
- Large bowl

Spread the newspaper over your work surface and place your poster board circle on top. Pour a few cups of flour into the bowl. Add one-half cup water and mix with your hands. The mixture should be a little thicker than the consistency of pancake batter. Add more flour, if necessary. Pour the mixture onto the circle and begin to create your craters. Poke and pull at your dough to make the surface hilly with craters. Add some smooth spots too. When you are finished, set your circle aside to dry. Does it look like the moon?

## So What's a Quadrant?

A *quadrant* is each of four quarters of a circle.

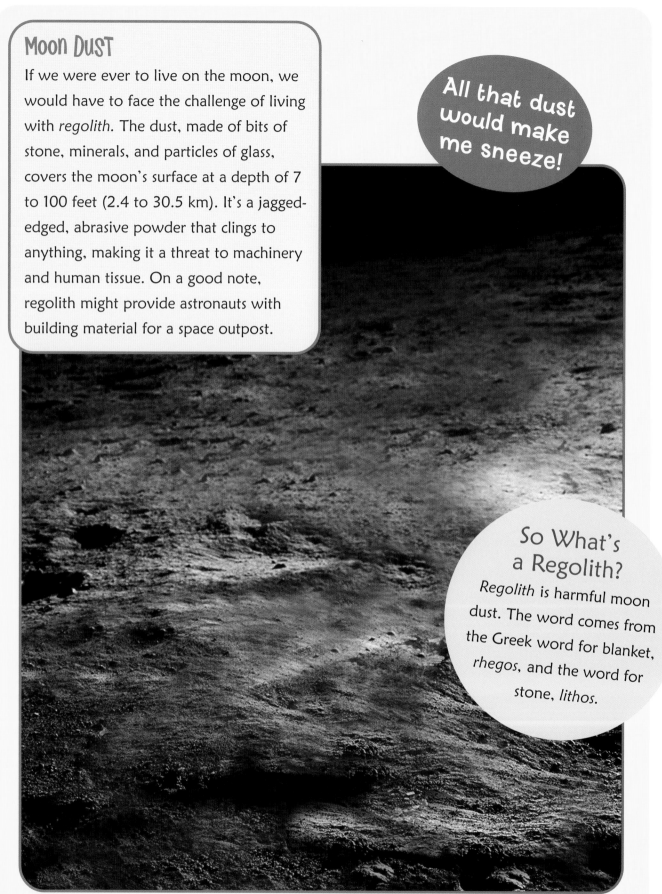

## Moon Dust

If we were ever to live on the moon, we would have to face the challenge of living with *regolith*. The dust, made of bits of stone, minerals, and particles of glass, covers the moon's surface at a depth of 7 to 100 feet (2.4 to 30.5 km). It's a jagged-edged, abrasive powder that clings to anything, making it a threat to machinery and human tissue. On a good note, regolith might provide astronauts with building material for a space outpost.

All that dust would make me sneeze!

### So What's a Regolith?

*Regolith* is harmful moon dust. The word comes from the Greek word for blanket, *rhegos*, and the word for stone, *lithos*.

*Regolith on the surface of the moon*

## Make It!

### Bubble Paint a Moon

The craters or holes on the moon are big and small. Some may only be as big as your fingernail. Others are very large. They were all created many years ago by meteors hitting the surface. Here's a way to picture the surface of the moon using something a little more gentle: bubbles.

**You Need**

- Newspaper
- Pie plate
- Water
- Dish detergent
- Teaspoon
- Spoon
- Tempera paint
- Drinking straw
- White finger-paint paper

Place newspaper over your work surface. Fill the pie plate with water. Add a couple of squirts of dish detergent and a teaspoon of tempera paint. Mix together with a spoon. Use the straw to blow bubbles on the surface of the water. Place the sheet of paper on top of the bubble-filled pie tin. Lift gently. Lay your paper on the newspaper to dry. Does it look like the craters on the moon? Experiment with other colors and other paper.

### Think about It!

Our moon is not the only moon in the sky. In fact, it is not even the only moon in our solar system. All the planets in our solar system have their own moons or natural satellites.

Uranus has 27 moons, including Desdemona, Juliet, Ariel, Titania, Oberon, Puck, and Miranda. Miranda looks like a jigsaw puzzle of pieces. The theory is that this moon broke apart millions of years ago. Gradually, gravity pulled the pieces back together, but the pieces can still be seen. Thanks to the Hubble Space Telescope, two more moons were seen and named Mab and Cupid.

## Picture of Neptune's Moons

Neptune has eight moons. Can you picture a planet with so many moons? Here's how to create a picture of Neptune's moons.

**You Need**

- Black paper
- Newspaper
- Toothbrush
- Water
- Watercolor paint set
- Paintbrush
- White watercolor paper
- Pencil
- Jar or coffee cup
- Glue stick
- Scissors

Prepare your night sky. Take your piece of black paper and lay it down on the newspaper. Dip your toothbrush into the water and then into the white paint. While holding your toothbrush in your hand, tap the handle with the other hand spattering little dots across the black paper. Those will be your stars. Set the paper aside to dry.

Let's create our planet Neptune next. Take your paintbrush, dip it in water, and paint over the surface of a sheet of watercolor paper with the water. Methane gas causes Neptune to appear blue, so now dip your paintbrush into the blue paint and paint on the wet paper in front of you, creating a blue wash. Set the paper aside to dry.

Create the moons of Neptune using another sheet of paper. The moons have a reddish tint to them. Paint the paper with water and then add the color red and other colors to the wet paper as in the previous step. Set the paper aside.

Draw Neptune on the dried blue paper. (You can use a jar or the bottom of a coffee as a guide.) Make the circle large, but make sure it will fit on the black sheet of paper. Add glue to the back of it and glue it to the center of the black paper. Cut out small moons from the other piece of watercolor paper. (Try using a smaller circle, like the bottom of a small cup.) Remember Neptune has eight moons. Can you cut out all eight and glue them around Neptune on the black paper and make them fit?

## Try This ↓

Create another picture with the 27 moons of Uranus. You will probably need a larger piece of black paper!

## Neptune's Triton

Of Neptune's eight moons, Triton is the most unusual. It orbits the planet in the opposite direction from all of Neptune's other moons. Triton has a frozen surface, but the ice on its surface acts like a greenhouse by magnifying the weak rays of the sun and heating the gas that lies below the surface. The result is slush and hot jets of gas that spout out from the icy surface.

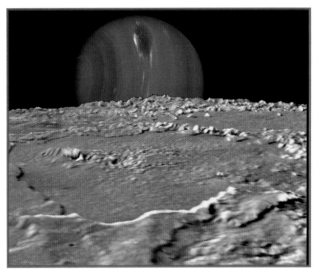

*The planet Neptune rises above its moon Triton.*

## Saturn's Titan

NASA's Cassini spacecraft has orbited Saturn since 2004 and has revealed some startling surpises about one of Saturn's moons. Titan has been found to look very much like Earth. It has mountains, dunes, riverbeds, volcanoes, clouds, and over seventy-five lakes; but the mountains are made of ice, the dunes are granules of ice coated with hydrocarbons, the volcanoes spit out methane and ammonia, and the lakes are filled with liquid methane that evaporates, forms clouds, and then rains back down to the surface.

Cassini also spotted a geyser on the moon shooting jets of water and icy particles hundreds of miles into the air. Scientists believe that liquid water may be under Titan's surface and might support forms of life.

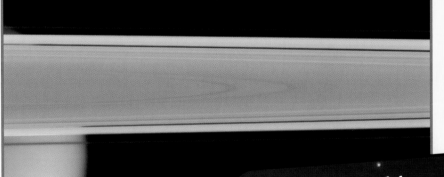

*Saturn's moon Titan seen behind Saturn's ring*

### The Constant Moon

Every night we can look up at the sky and see the constant moon orbiting our Earth. We can rely on its position and its phases, but not everything in space is so constant. We'll see in the next chapter that there are other objects that do not maintain the same position in the sky. Sometimes they even collide with planets. Sometimes they put on a spectacular show. Are you ready?

# Comets, Asteroids, Meteoroids, and Other Things Flying Through Space

**P**lanets, moons, and stars are not alone. There are comets, asteroids, and meteoroids that are also flying through space. *Comets* are bodies of ice that measure from about 3,000 feet (914.4 m) to over sixty miles (96.5 km) across. *Asteroids* are made of stone, are odd-shaped, and usually measure about 3,000 feet (914.4 m) to over 600 miles (965.6 km) across, but some are the size of tiny dust particles. *Meteoroids* are pieces of comets or asteroids and can be the size of a dust particle to more than 300 feet (91.4 m) across. Those are all "natural" objects. There are also man-made objects that are flying high in space. We'll explore them all.

## So What's a Comet?

A *comet* is a celestial body of ice and dust that travels in an elliptical orbit.

## So What's an Asteroid?

An *asteroid* is a small celestial body made of rock that orbits the sun.

## So What's a Meteoroid?

A *meteroid* is a small chunk broken off from an asteroid or comet. When it enters the earth's atmosphere and can be seen, it is called a *meteor* or a shooting star.

# Face of SPACE

## Sir Edmond Halley

*"This sight . . . is by far the noblest astronomy affords."—Edmond Halley*

Sir Edmond Halley, most famous for his discovery of the comet that was named for him, was born in 1656. When he first saw the comet in 1705, he predicted, using Newton's laws of motion and mathematical formulas, that it would again be seen in the year 1758. As predicted the comet did appear that year and it became known to scientists as comet Halley.

Sir Edmond Halley, unfortunately, did not live to see his prediction come true. He died in 1742.

Halley also helped increase our understanding of trade winds, tides, cartography, and naval navigation. He theorized that Earth was made of concentric spheres and that each of these inner planets might contain life. That theory was proven not to be true, but could make for a great science fiction story!

### Mark Your Calendar

Comet Halley was last viewed in 1986. The average period of the comet's orbit is every seventy-six years, meaning we won't be able to view comet Halley again until 2062.

I can't wait that long!

*Comet Hale-Bopp*

## Comet Hale-Bopp

On July 23, 1995, two observers spotted a fuzzy object in the constellation Sagittarius. The two observers were Alan Hale—who has a PhD in astronomy and has observed over 200 comets in his lifetime—and Thomas Bopp—an amateur astronomer who was observing the sky during a "star party." Within minutes of each other they had both called in their discovery to the worldwide clearing-house for comet discoveries in Cambridge, Massachusetts, so both their names were given to the new comet. The comet was the farthest comet discovered by amateurs. It appeared to be 1,000 times brighter than comet Halley. The comet became bright enough to see without the aid of a telescope by 1997 and was visible until April/May of that year.

## What Is a Comet Made of?

Every day scientists make discoveries that impact our knowledge of the universe. In March 2006, NASA scientists discovered evidence of ice and fire in comet particles. It had been a common belief that comets mostly contain ice, dust, and gases.

The NASA program, STARDUST, retrieved particles from within 150 miles (241.4 km) of the comet WILD 2 in 2004. The particles showed high-temperature materials from the coldest part of our solar system. The discovery alters the belief that comets are basically dust, ice, and gases. They may be more complex than that.

One of the materials found by STARDUST is *olivine*, a material also found in Hawaiian green beach sand. Olivine is made of iron, magnesium, and other elements. The samples also contained other high-temperature materials, such as calcium and aluminum. Astronomers are constantly revising their beliefs by making new discoveries that are possible with new technology.

Gas Tail

Dust Tail

### The Comet Tail

Animals aren't the only things with tails. Comets can also have tails. That's the trail we see behind the comet as it moves. There are two types of comet tails: gas and dust. Gas tails tend to be more common but less bright than dust tails. Unfortunately, the increase in light pollution makes comets harder to see and their tails even more difficult to spot.

# Experiment with Making a Comet Nucleus

Here's an experiment that follows the theory that comets mostly contain ice, dust, and gases.

**You Need**

- Mixing bowl
- 2 plastic bags
- 1 cup water
- ½ cup dirt
- Large spoon
- Spray bottle of window cleaner
- ½ teaspoon corn syrup
- 1 squirt graphite (can be purchased in a hobby shop)
- 1 cup dry ice (check your local ice-cream store)
- 2 heavy-duty garbage bags
- Hammer
- Insulated gloves

Line the mixing bowl with the two plastic bags. Add one cup water and one-half cup dirt and stir with your large spoon. Like dirty snowballs, comets are mostly made of ice. The dirt represents the silicates found in comets. Add three sprays of window cleaner, which represent the ammonia in comets. Next, add corn syrup and graphite. Corn syrup represents organic hydrocarbons and graphite represents the black carbon material found in comets. Stir until mixed. Have a grown up place one cup dry ice inside two garbage bags and crush it with a hammer until there are only small chunks left. (Comets are about 30% dry ice.) Stir dry ice into the bowl. Pick up the grocery bags while wearing the gloves and form the mixture into a round ball.

# Comet Shatters and Is Captured on Film

The Hubble Space Telescope has captured the breakup of Comet Schwassmann-Wachmann in deep space. Comet Schwassmann-Wachmann orbits the sun every five years and three months and was first discovered in 1930. In 1995 astronomers witnessed the initial breakup of the comet into four pieces. Comets heat up when they get close to the sun.

Trapped gases sometimes explode out. Scientists took the still images gathered from HST and combined them into a time-lapse movie that shows the comet shattering into more than thirty-three pieces, the smallest of them roughly the size of a house, according to scientists. Look in the resource section for a link to dramatic online pictures.

## Shooting Stars

Once in a while you might see what looks like a star streak across the sky. These streaks are not actually stars, but *meteors*. Stars are huge balls of gas that glow in the night sky. They look very small to us because they are very far away. A meteor is a streak of light caused by a *meteoroid*, which is a solid ball of rock, metal, or ice that is very small. In fact, a meteoroid might only be the size of a pea, which has broken off from a comet or asteroid.

When the meteoroid enters the atmosphere of our planet, it vaporizes in a flash of light. A *meteorite* is a meteoroid that has struck the Earth. Large meteoroids can leave large craters or holes in the Earth. You can see meteorites at local rock shops or natural history museums.

## Hairy Comets?

The word *comet* comes from the Greek word for "hair." Ancient people thought that comets looked a bit like the heads of women with long hair. People also thought they looked like swords, which led to some of the fear associated with them. It was thought that comets were messages sent by the gods and warned of war and plagues. Church bells would ring to try to ward off the evil that came with the comets. Of course, we know that bad things also occurred when there were not comets in the sky, but many ancient people didn't notice that.

# Try This ↓

## Watch a Meteor Shower Show

It is such a treat to be out on a dark-sky night and count "shooting stars" flashing across the sky. There are times during the year when you might be able to see 10 to 100 per hour, depending on the year and the event. These events of increased meteor activity are called *meteor showers*. They are named after the constellation from which the meteors appear to be falling. For example, the Perseid meteor shower is named after the constellation Perseus, where the meteors seem to begin. The showers vary each year. Some years they're more intense and in other years a bit quieter. Look at the calendar in the Resources section for approximate times when the showers occur. Here are some viewing tips:

**You Need**

- Chairs
- Insect repellent
- Red flashlight
- Blankets
- Snacks

When you know that you will be able to view a meteor shower in your area, treat it like the Fourth of July. Bring out comfortable chairs, insect repellent, blankets, and snacks. Drive away from any city lights to a dark-sky area in the direction of the constellation. Drive north to view the Leonids and northeast for the Perseid. Let your eyes adapt to the darkness. Once you can see all the stars of the Little Dipper, your eyes have adjusted. Make yourself comfortable and begin watching the sky. You'll see streaks of light across the sky. They will look like stars falling from the heavens. How many can you count in an hour?

Record the data from your meteor shower watch into a journal. Write down the hours you watched the sky and how many meteors you observed each hour. Watch the news and see how your data compares. Find a web site in the resource section on the meteor shower to find out more up-to-date information.

That's awesome!

*Meteor Crater, Arizona*

## Field Trip to Arizona

Travel to Arizona and view Meteor Crater. It was the first crater to be identified as an impact crater. It was determined that an asteroid about eighty feet (23.4 m) in diameter crashed into Earth between 20,000 and 50,000 years ago. An explosive force more than twenty million tons (18,143,694.8 metric tons) of TNT left the huge crater behind.

The crater measures about three-fourths of a mile (1.2 km) in diameter and is 700 feet (210 m) deep.

Visitors to the crater will find a great visitor center that includes an interactive learning center. A movie, *Collisions and Impacts*, is shown throughout the day and a gift shop is on site. Turn to the Resources section for details.

## Huge Crater Found in Egypt

A huge crater was found in the Gilf Kebir region in southwestern Egypt's Sahara Desert that is even larger than Meteor Crater. The crater was named *Kebira*, which is Arabic for large. It is about nineteen miles (31 km) wide, which dwarfs Meteor Crater, and is twice as big as the second largest Saharan crater.

It was discovered in satellite images by Boston University researchers. Scientists believe that the meteor that caused the crater was itself three-fourths of a mile (1.2 km) wide and most likely caused an event that destroyed everything for hundreds of miles around the impact site.

## Experiment with Impact Exploration

Let's see firsthand how these craters are formed when a meteorite crashes to Earth. We'll see how size and speed affect the size and shape of the craters.

**You Need**

- Aluminum baking pan
- Flour
- Cocoa
- Several pebbles of different sizes
- Ruler
- Pencil
- Paper

Fill the pan with one-and-one-quarter to one-and-one-half inches (3–4 cm) of flour and place it on the floor. Sprinkle a bit of cocoa on the top. Pick out one of the smallest pebbles and drop it into the pan from about eye level. What size crater did it form? Use your ruler to measure the crater. Pick out a larger pebble and drop it as you did the first. Is the crater larger or smaller? Record your data on your paper. Try the experiment one more time with a larger pebble. What do you think will happen?

Now let's take a look at speed. Pick out three pebbles that are roughly the same size. Smooth out the flour and sprinkle a little more cocoa on the surface. Drop the first pebble from about knee high. Look at the crater it formed. Drop the second pebble from about eye level. How does that crater compare? Hold your arm high above your head and drop the third pebble. How does the third crater compare? How does speed affect the size and shape of the craters?

### Turquoise

Many Native Americans call the gem *turquoise* the "sky stone," a little piece of the sky that has fallen to Earth.

# Face of SPACE

## Maria Mitchell

*"We have a hunger of the mind, which asks for knowledge of all around us, and the more we gain, the more is our desire; the more we see, the more we are capable of seeing."— Maria Mitchell*

Maria Mitchell was blessed to be the daughter of an astronomer who encouraged her interest in science. She grew up on Nantucket Island off the coast of Massachusetts, where women often managed things at home while their husbands were at sea. Unlike women on the mainland, Nantucket women had more freedom. Maria started school in 1822, already knowing how to read. When she was seventeen, she started a school of her own for girls, ages six and up.

Maria became the librarian for Nantucket's Athenaeum Library and assisted her father in his observatory. In 1847, Maria took time out from a party to gaze at the stars with her telescope. She found a hazy light near the North Star that she identified as a comet. Maria was awarded a gold medal from the King of Denmark for being the first person to find a "telescopic comet," meaning the comet could only be seen through a telescope. The medal read *"Non Frustra Signorum Orbitus Speculamur ot Ortus,"* which translates to "Not in vain do we watch the setting and the rising of stars."

Maria Mitchell went on to teach astronomy at Vassar College in New York and became recognized as the first woman astronomer in the United States. She even has a crater on the moon named after her!

## The Asteroid Belt

In 1801, Guiseppe Piazzi looked up in the sky and saw what he thought was a comet. He watched it and found that, unlike a comet, it had an orbit, like a small planet. He named it Ceres, after the Sicilian goddess of grain. Over the coming years, three other small celestial bodies were identified. By the end of the nineteenth century, several hundred of these small bodies were found.

Scientists identified these objects as asteroids. We now know that there is a high concentration of asteroids between the planets of Mars and Jupiter in some 20 million miles of space. This asteroid belt is home to thousands of asteroids, roughly 90–95% of all the asteroids in our

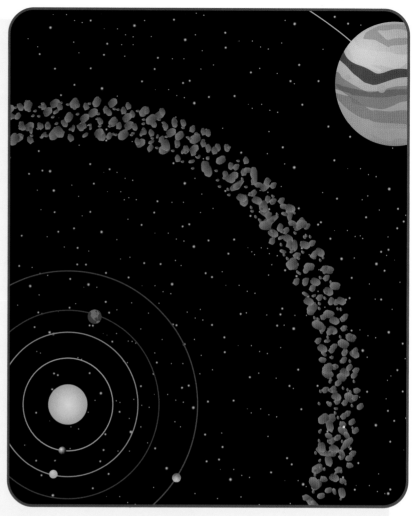

solar system. Scientists believe that these chunks of rock are actually the remains of a planet that never completely developed.

You can't see asteroids without a telescope or a good pair of binoculars. Most of the asteroids are in stable orbits, meaning they stay in their orbit and don't fly freely through space, but once in a while Jupiter's gravitational pull can take hold of one and pull it out of its orbit. When that happens, the asteroid is on a random path. There is a threat that one of these could possibly hit Earth. For this reason, scientists track these Near-Earth Objects or NEOs.

## Try This

If you're planning a visit to Nantucket, Massachusetts, head over to the Maria Mitchell Association at 4 Vestal Street. You can visit Maria Mitchell's house, investigate some of the island's natural history at the Association's Natural Science Museum at the Hinchman House and the Aquarium, and lastly, explore the skies at the Loines Observatory and Vestal Street Observatory. Just like Maria, you can gaze up into the Nantucket sky and maybe you'll even make a discovery! It's a great place to spend the day and the night!

## Satellites

Not of all the objects sailing through the sky are natural; some are man made. We rely on these man-made objects, called *satellites*, for our communication, space exploration, weather forecasting, navigation, research, and spying on other countries. Cable television relies on satellites to distribute its transmissions. Newspapers and news services transmit their text using satellites. Global positioning devices (GPS) that are now found in many cars also rely on satellites.

Man-made satellites are created to orbit the Earth, just as our moon does, but a bit closer. All satellites have some basic components: solar panels to generate electricity; sensors to measure temperature, wavelength, longitude, and latitude; and antennae to send signals to Earth.

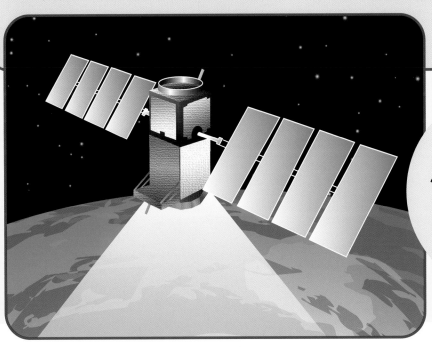

### So What's a Satellite?

A *satellite* is a celestial body that orbits the earth or other planets.

## Space Junk

The former Soviet Union launched the world's first satellite, *Sputnik*, in 1957 and began the world's race to be first in space. Satellites made today are more complex, but all contribute to the space junk that orbits our planet. Many of the satellites that are launched outlive their usefulness and continue to float through space above Earth. There are approximately 26,000 objects, including old satellites, rocket motors, and other rocket parts that are currently tracked as space junk.

## So What's a Sputnik?

*Sputnik* is a Russian word for satellite and was the name of the very first man-made satellite. The word literally means "fellow-traveler."

## The Satillite Launch

Satellites are launched into space on a rocket or on a space shuttle. It is important to pick the right time to launch the satellite into space, when weather is safe and all other conditions are optimum. This perfect time is called the *launch window*. If the space shuttle is delivering the satellite, the launch window secures a time when it will be safe for the astronauts on the shuttle. If weather is bad or there is something wrong with the shuttle, the trip will be postponed to another launch window.

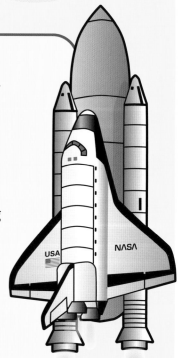

# Face of SPACE

## Nahide Craig

You've seen that there are many different careers for people interested in space. Some study stars, some become astronauts, and others, like Nahide Craig, combine their studies with their other interests.

Nahide wanted to be an archeologist when she was young. She wanted to dig into the earth to look for ancient things and try to solve the puzzle of what life was like in ancient times. Instead she became an astronomer and is still studying objects that

are even more ancient than anything we can dig up on Earth.

When her son and daughter entered school, Nahide became deeply involved with their education and served as the school district's science adviser. She began to combine her astronomy work at Space Sciences Laboratory with various NASA science education projects, which included developing appropriate materials for science teachers.

### Flying through the Dark Sky

Can you imagine all of the things that are flying through space when you look up at a dark night sky? The night seems so quiet and the stars sit in the darkness twinkling like little beacons. Could you imagine all of the activity that is going on high above our heads? Turn the page and begin to imagine yourself among the stars like the astronauts who step into their spacesuits and take incredible journeys.

# Space Race

Not long ago space travel was just a dream. In fact, you might be able to find a book in your library about space that was written before space travel existed. You don't even have to look very far. Space travel is less than fifty years old. The space program has made so many discoveries since that time that many books are already out-of-date. Every day scientists are analyzing new data and revamping theories. The space program has changed how we look at the universe. Look at the following time line and see how the United States and the Soviet Union (Russia) competed in the race into space. Decide for yourself if the competition between the United States and Soviet Union strengthened the space program or weakened it.

# Space Race To The Moon Timeline

**1957** USSR (Russia) launches Sputnik 1, the first man-made satellite.

**1958** United States launches Explorer 1, the first U.S. satellite.

**1959** Soviet probes, Luna 1, Luna 2, and Luna 3 make headlines.

**1960** Unites States launches the first weather satellite, Tiros 1.

**1961** In April, Soviet Vostok 1 carries the first man in space, cosmonaut Yuri A. Gagarin.

**1961** In May, Alan Shepard, Jr., becomes the first U.S. astronaut in space in Mercury capsule Freedom 7.

**1962** In February, American John Glenn, Jr., becomes the first man to orbit Earth.

**1962** In July, the U.S. satellite Telstar 1 beams the first live telecast from the U.S. to Europe.

**1962** In December, the U.S. Mariner 2 flies past Venus.

**1963** The Soviets put the first woman in space, cosmonaut Valentina Tereshkova. She orbits Earth 48 times.

**1964** U.S. lunar spacecraft, Ranger 7, relays the first close-up photos of the moon.

**1964** In November, U.S. Mariner 4 returns with data about Mars.

**1965** In March, cosmonaut Alexi Leonov makes the first space walk.

**1965** In June, U.S. astronauts make their first space walk.

**1966** The Soviet Luna 9 soft-lands on the moon in February.

**1966** In June, the U.S. spacecraft soft-lands on the moon.

**1968** The U.S. launches Apollo 8, the first manned spacecraft to orbit the moon.

# Face of SPACE

## John Glenn

John Glenn was the first American to orbit our planet in space. He began his career as a pilot for the U.S. Marine Corps. After flying in both World War II and the Korean War, Glenn was assigned to NASA (National Aeronautics and Space Administration) in 1957. He piloted the Friendship 7 spacecraft on February 20, 1962. Glenn said of the flight, "I don't know what you could say about a day in which you have seen four beautiful sunsets."

Glenn became so popular that he ran for the United States Senate and was elected in 1974. That didn't stop his career in space travel. In 1998 at age seventy-seven, he became the oldest person to ever fly in space when he flew the space shuttle, *Discovery*, on a research mission. Glenn retired from the Senate in 1999.

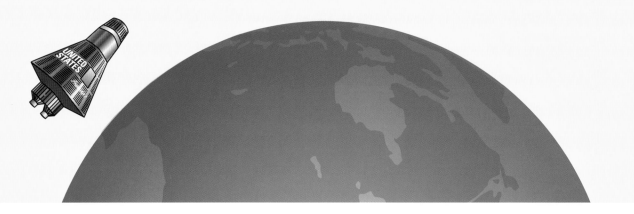

## Astronaut Training

There have been many astronauts that have felt the wonder that John Glenn felt back in 1962. They all prepare years for their trip into space, many at an astronaut training school in Texas. They step into flight simulators to learn how to control a spaceship and find control panels with hundreds of buttons to press. They learn what it feels like to be weightless by training underwater, which is the closest thing on Earth to weightlessness. They also learn how to keep comfortable and stay alive in their spacesuit.

*Astronaut exercising in space*

## Presidential Mandate

In 2004 President George W. Bush issued a mandate "Vision for Space Exploration" that called for the development of a new spacecraft to carry humans to the moon by the year 2020 and eventually send them to Mars. The mandate also calls for building a new space station and the retirement of the space shuttle by 2010.

*I'd like to go to the moon!*

## Think about It!

In 1986 Christa McAuliffe, a high-school social studies teacher, stepped out of her classroom and into space travel. Out of 11,500 applicants from teachers, doctors, authors, and many others, Christa was chosen to be the first teacher in space. She became the first civilian, or non-astronaut, to become part of a space mission. Although her mission on the *Challenger* ended tragically, Christa helped rekindle excitement for the space program. Would you have applied?

# Face of SPACE

## Sally Ride

*"When you're getting ready to launch into space, you're sitting on a big explosion waiting to happen."—Sally Ride*

Sally Ride was the first woman to orbit Earth. She was born in 1951 and, as a young girl, wanted to be a professional tennis player. She competed on the junior tennis circuit and then went on to Stanford University where she earned four degrees: a BA in English, a BS in Physics, a MS in Physics, and a PhD in Physics. She applied to the space program after seeing an ad in the newspaper. More than 8,000 people applied, and of the thirty-five accepted, only six were women. In 1983 Ride became the first women to orbit our planet. When she left the space program in 1987 she joined the faculty of her alma mater, Stanford University.

# Try This

## Write to Sally Ride

Do you have specific questions about space travel you'd like to ask an astronaut? Here's how you might be able to have them answered for you.

**You Need**

- Pencil
- 2 envelopes
- 2 postage stamps
- Paper

Dr. Sally Ride, Director
California Space Institute
University of California at San Diego
La Jolla, CA 92093

Address one envelope to yourself and place a U.S. postage stamp in the right-hand corner. Address the other to Astronaut Sally Ride and place a stamp in the right-hand corner of that envelope.

> *Dr. Sally Ride, Director*
> *California Space Institute*
> *University of California at San Diego*
> *La Jolla, CA 92093*

Begin writing your letter. Print clearly or type it out on the computer. Dear Dr. Sally Ride:

The next step is to write the body of your letter. Think about what you would like to ask. Keep your letter short by asking only one or two questions. When you're ready to close your letter, it is appropriate to end with Regards, or Sincerely, followed by your name.

Fold your letter carefully and place it in the envelope addressed to Sally Ride. Include the envelope that you addressed to yourself so that she can place her response in it and mail it back to you.

Be patient when waiting for a response. Dr. Ride is not able to respond to everyone with her busy schedule. If she does respond to you, keep your letter in a safe place. You might want to take it to school to show your teacher.

# The Spacesuit

The spacesuit is the key ingredient in the survival of every astronaut. It is like its own body-size spaceship and has several thin but strong layers to protect the astronaut from the heat and cold of space and from tiny meteoroids that the astronaut might encounter outside of the ship. A layer of spandex is worn next to the body containing tubes filled with water that the astronaut can cool or heat. There is also a urine-collecting device for later transfer and an in-suit drink bag that holds drinking water. A cap, often called the *Snoopy cap* and worn under the helmet, holds a radio microphone and an earpiece. Lights in the helmet help the astronaut see in the dark.

# Food in Flight

In the early days of space exploration, foods taken into space were mainly packaged in tubes. Astronauts inserted a straw into the tube and then into their mouths, just like drinking soda. Other foods were freeze-dried and made into tiny snacks. Later other foods were dehydrated and could be re-hydrated with water when the astronaut was ready to eat. The dehydration process made it possible for astronauts to eat foods such as turkey and gravy, shrimp cocktail, fruit cocktail, and cream-of-chicken soup. Meals on Apollo flights included cornflakes, scrambled eggs, bacon squares, and chocolate pudding.

## Experiment with Space Food

The variety of foods expanded on the recent space shuttle program to include seventy-four different foods and twenty beverages. Here's how you can try your hand at rehydrating food like an astronaut.

### You Need

- 1 package instant pudding
- Calculator
- Measuring spoons
- Plastic zip-lock sandwich bags
- 1 package nonfat dry milk
- Water
- Spoon

Look at the package of instant pudding and read the number of servings per package. Use your calculator to figure out how much of each ingredient you will need for only one serving. Measure the amount of pudding mix needed and place it in the sandwich bag. Add the appropriate amount of nonfat dry milk needed. (Read the package directions for one serving.) Seal the bag and shake the ingredients together. Add the correct amount of water to the bag, seal well, and knead with your fingers to mix well. Leave the pudding a few minutes to thicken then eat with your spoon. Can you think of other foods that you eat regularly that need to be rehydrated?

## Chef Rachael Ray's Food Heads to Space

Rachael Ray, host of *30-Minute Meals* and the *Rachael Ray Show*, has prepared three meals for NASA, the very first meals in the space program to include a garnish. The meals, including Spicy Thai Chicken, were prepared at NASA with specific measurements and then freeze-dried for five days before packaging them up for the mission. Once aboard, the astronauts will rehydrate the meals and enjoy a tasty treat from a great chef!

## So What's Rehydrate?

*Rehydrate* means to add moisture to something that has been dehydrated in order to return it to its natural state.

**NASA Spin-offs**

Has the space program touched you personally? Of course it has. The space program has greatly enhanced our lives here on Earth. Research and development for the space program has been spun off to reach us in many ways. For example, your sneakers might have technology to improve shock absorption that was first developed for the boots worn on the moon. Here are just a few other spin-offs that were developed that your family might be using right now.

- Fogless ski goggles
- Dust busters
- Food packaging
- Cool sportswear
- Smoke detectors
- Flat panel televisions
- Self-adjusting sunglasses
- Enriched baby food
- Portable coolers
- Fire-resistant material

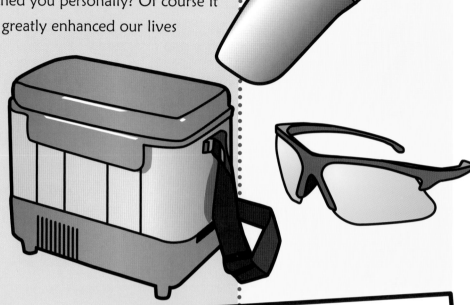

# The Daily  Globe

# Astronaut Runs Boston Marathon

What if you qualify for the Boston Marathon, but you can't be there because you are 210 miles (338 km) above the course in a space station? You run on a treadmill, like Astronaut Sunita Williams did in April of 2007. Williams taped her entry number, 14,000, to the front of her treadmill, wore her Boston Red Sox socks, harnessed herself in, and took off running at 10:00 AM (EST) just like every other runner in the marathon, including her sister Dina. Both sisters completed the marathon in just less than four and half hours, 210 vertical miles apart.

*Astronaut training in space*

## Make It!

### A Rocket

Do you think you may want to be an astronaut when you are older? If so, building rockets is a great way to start. Here's how to make a simple rocket that you can shoot off safely. When you master this one, there are others you can try and there are many rocket-building competitions when you enter middle school and high school.

**You Need**

- Grownup
- Pencil
- Paper
- Ruler
- Scissors

- A 35-mm film container without cap
- Clear tape
- Open outdoor area
- Bottle of water
- Alka Seltzer tablets

Draw a line down a sheet of paper creating a rectangle about 6 x 11 inches. Cut it out using your scissors. Wrap the rectangle around the film container creating a long tube with the canister on the bottom of the tube. Tape it together. Create your nose cone by drawing a circle on a sheet of paper roughly six inches in diameter. Cut it out and fold it into a cone shape. Tape the edge of the cone to the rocket tube. Draw four triangle fins to tape to the bottom of the rocket. This will enable your rocket to stand on its own. To launch your rocket, begin by lifting up the rocket tube and filling the film canister about two-thirds with water. Place the rocket on the ground outside. Place one-half Alka Seltzer tablet in the water. Replace the rocket tube and stand back several feet from your rocket. In just a few seconds your rocket will take off!

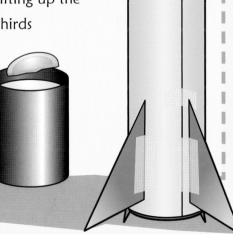

# Face of SPACE

## Dr. Wernher von Braun

Wernher von Braun was born in Germany in 1912. He grew up reading the science fiction of Jules Verne and H. G. Wells. When he was twelve years old, he conducted his first rocket experiment. He took a coaster wagon and fastened to it a half dozen of the biggest skyrockets he could find. He lit the rockets and watched the coaster careen wildly around "trailing a tail of fire like a comet." Dr. von Braun remembered it performing beyond his wildest dreams.

When he grew older he attempted to read Hermann Oberth's nonfiction book, *The Rocket to the Interplanetary Spaces*, but found it too difficult. His teacher advised him to study physics and math, which he did. Ironically, it was with Oberth and other scientists that von Braun later developed the German V2 rocket. It was the first rocket capable of reaching space. At the end of World War II, von Braun led the top German scientists out of Germany to the United States, where he led the development of rockets for space exploration and the military. He joined NASA and became the director of the Marshall Space Flight Center in Huntsville, Alabama. In 1975 von Braun received the United States National Medal of Science. He is generally regarded as the father of the U.S. space program.

# The Future of Space Travel

Just as previous generations thought sending a spaceship to the moon was impossible, it might be difficult for us to believe that space travel to distant galaxies might be in our future. How could we possibly leave this world and travel trillions of miles to other solar systems? Rockets would have to travel much faster and we have not developed a rocket that can travel as fast as the speed of light yet. With our current rockets, space travel to even our closest star, Alpha Centauri, would take many years. If we sent a sixteen-year-old astronaut to Alpha Centauri, he or she would arrive as a senior citizen, too old to make the return trip to Earth. It would take hundreds of years or maybe thousands of years, to travel to other solar systems. Impossible? We've seen many things we thought impossible become possible. Who knows what lies ahead for the future of space travel?

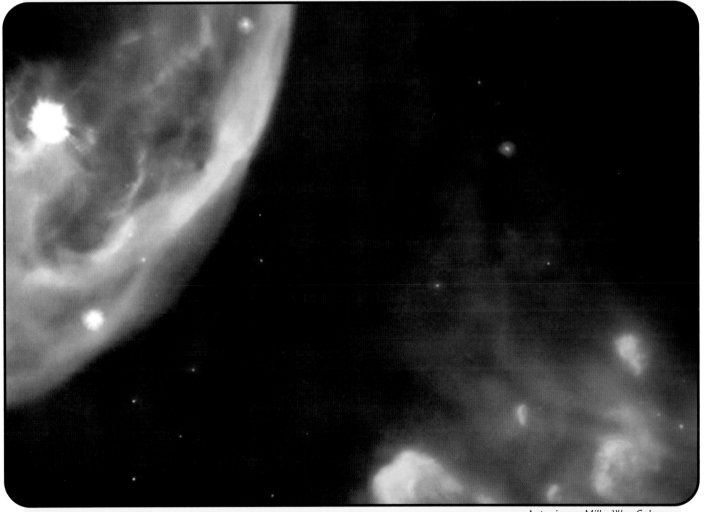

*A star in our Milky Way Galaxy*

# Resources

**Books:**

Aldrin, Buzz. *Reaching for the Moon.* New York: HarperCollins, 2005.

Berman, Bob. *Secrets of the Night Sky.* New York: Morrow, 1995.

Crelin, Bob. *There Once Was a Sky Full of Stars.* Cambridge, Massachusetts: Sky Publishing Corp., 2004

Dwyer, Mindy. *Aurora: A Tale of the Northern Lights.* Anchorage, AK: Alaska Northwest books, 1997.

Ehlert, Lois, *Moon Rope*, New York: Voyager Books, 2003

Glenn, John. *Liftoff: A Photobiography of John Glenn.* New York: National Geographic Children's Books, 2006

Hendrie, Michael. *The Times Night Sky 2006: A Month-to-Month Guide to the Stars, Planets, Moon, and Major Meteor Showers.* New York: Times Books, 2005 (look for the current edition in your bookstore)

Kinsey-Warnock, Natalie. *The Fiddler of the Northern Lights.* New York: Dutton Children's books, 1996.

Marriott, Lee. *The Universe: Images From The Hubble Telescope.* Secaucus, New Jersey: Chartwell Books, 2004

Paratore, Coleen M., *Catching the Sun.* Boston, Charlesbridge, 2008.

Priceman, Marjorie. *How to Make an Apple Pie and See the World.* New York: Dragonfly Books, 1996

Rey, H. A., *Find the Constellations.* New York: Houghton Mifflin, 1976.

Rey, H.A., *The Stars.* New York: Houghton Mifflin, 1976.

Ride, Sally. *Exploring Our Solar System.* New York: Crown Books for Young Readers, 2003.

Sis, Peter. *Starry Messenger.* New York: Farrar, Straus and Giroux (BYR), 1996

Watson, Clyde. *Midnight Moon.* New York: Putnam, 1979

Winter, Jeanette. *Follow The Drinking Gourd.* New York: Dragonfly Books, 1992

**Web Sites:**

Find out more about the science of light at: www.learner.org/teacherslab/science/light/

Celebrate National Dark Sky Week: www.ndsw.org/

Tune into Earth and Sky Radio at www.earthsky.org/shows/?year=2006

Check out NASA's Astronomy Picture of the Day at http://antwrp.gsfc.nasa.gov/apod/archivepix.html

Purchase a lens at: Surplus Shed has inexpensive educational http://www.earthsky.org/shows/?year=2006 lenses. www.surplusshed.com/pages/category/educationaloptics_1.html

Edmund Scientific sells lenses too. Check out their website at http://www.edsci.com, and request a mail-order catalog.

Take a virtual tour of the solar system at www.nationalgeographic.com/solarsystem/splash.html

Check out NASA's site on the solar system at http://solarsystem.nasa.gov/index.cfm

Here's another multimedia virtual tour of the solar system: www.nineplanets.org

Energy Kid's Page: www.eia.doe.gov/kids/energyfacts/index.html

News and Information about the Sun-Earth Environment: www.spaceweather.com

Find out more about sunspots at this NASA site. http://science.nasa.gov/ssl/pad/solar/sunspots.htm

Check out NASA's Eclipse Page for some awesome pictures and information.
http://sunearth.gsfc.nasa.gov/eclipse/solar.html

Learn more about Columbus and Celestial Navigation at www.columbusnavigation.com/cn.shtml

Here's a listing of all 88 constellations:
http://homepage.mac.com/kvmagruder/bcp/aster/constellations/index.html

Take a look at the reviews the 6th graders at Keystone Central School District wrote about Van Gogh's
  Starry Night at www.kcsd.k12.pa.us/~projects/critic/student.html
Investigate images of the sky at:
  http://images.google.com/images?hl=en&lr=&q=Starry%20Night%20&sa=N&tab=wi
  http://www.austindavid.com/gallery/paintings/images/moon.jpg
  http://www.stec.art.pl/imgl/22x.jpg
  http://www.flutterbyearomatics.com/flutterpooch/snoods/starry_night.jpg
See photos of the Moon's surface at http://zebu.uoregon.edu/~soper/Moon/surface.html
Here are some pictures of the lunar cycle: http://aa.usno.navy.mil/faq/docs/moon_phases.html
Take a look at the moons of Uranus at www.dustbunny.com/afk/planets/uranus/uranusmoons.html
Here's a page about the moons of Neptune: www.kidsastronomy.com/neptune/moons.htm
Check out Comet Halley at www.nineplanets.org/halley.html
There are a lot of sites with images of the great comet of 1997, Comet Hale-Bopp. Here's NASA's site:
  www2.jpl.nasa.gov/comet/index.html
Here's some photos of Comet Schwassmann-Wachmann:
  http://www.thunderbolts.info/tpod/2006/arch06/060505cometbreakup.htm
Check out Gary Kronk's Comets and Meteors Observing Calendar at
  www.serve.com/wh6ef/comets/meteors/calendar.html
For more on meteor showers see StarDate at http://stardate.org/nightsky/meteors/
Visit Meteor Crater in Arizona. Here's the site for more information. www.meteorcrater.com/index.htm
Learn more about rockets and rocket-building contests at www.rocketcontest.org/
Astronaut Photography of Earth http://eol.jsc.nasa.gov/info/use.htm

## Space Camps

### Alabama
Huntsville: U.S. Space and Rocket Center, 800-63-SPACE, www.spacecamp.com

### Arizona
Tucson: Astronomy Camp, 800-BEAT-ASU, www.astronomycamp.org/

### California
Berkley: Sally Ride Science Camp for Girls, 800-548-6612, www.educationunlimited.com/sallyride/science.html
Idyllwild: AstroCamp, 800-645-1423, http://www.guideddiscoveries.org/

### Florida
Daytona Beach: Embry-Riddle Summer Academy, 800-359-4550, www.erau.edu/db/summer/summeracademy.html
Boca Raton, Miami, Plantation, and Weston: FasTracKids, 561-483-4105,
  http://locsystem.fastrackids.com/franchisee.asp?gymid=23
*Kennedy Space Center: Camp Kennedy Space Center www.kennedyspacecenter.com/educatorsParents/camp.asp
Lakeland: Destination Aviation, 863-644-2431, www.flairmuseum.org/content/museum/main.asp?section=museum

### Kansas
Hutchinson: Cosmosphere Programs, including TAKEOFF, 800-397-0330, www.cosmo.org/

### New York
Alfred: Alfred University Astronomy Camp, 607-871-2612, www.alfred.edu/summer/

## Places to Visit
### Planetariums /United States
#### Alabama
Huntsville Planetarium, Von Braun Astronomical Society, www.vbas.org/index.cfm

#### Alaska
Juneau: Marie Drake Planetarium, www.mariedrakeplanetarium.org/JUNEAU%20STARS.html

#### Arizona
Flagstaff: Lowell Observatory, www.lowell.edu/

Phoenix: Planetarium Project, Arizona Science Center, www.azscience.org/planetarium_2.php

Tucson: Flandrau Science Center and Planetarium, www.flandrau.org/

#### California
Berkeley: William K. Holt Planetarium Lawrence Hall of Science,
www.lawrencehallofscience.org/planetarium/

Chico: Roth Planetarium, California State University – Chico, http://rigel.csuchico.edu/roth/roth.html

Los Angeles: Planetarium, Griffith Observatory, www.griffithobs.org/Planetarium.html

Oakland: Rotary Chabot Planetarium, Chabot Observatory & Science Center, www.chabotspace.org/

Redding: Schreder Planetarium, Shasta County. Office of Education, www.schrederplanetarium.com/

San Diego: Reuben H. Fleet Space Theater and Science Center, www.rhfleet.org/

San Francisco: Alexander Morrison Planetarium, California Academy of Sciences,
www.calacademy.org/planetarium/

San Francisco: Charles F. Hagar Planetarium, San Francisco St. University,
http://cannon.sfsu.edu/~lwilliam/planet/shows.html

Santa Barbara: Gladwin Planetarium, Santa Barbara Museum of Natural History,
www.sbnature.org/education/planetarium/

#### Colorado
Boulder: Wallace Fiske Planetarium, University of Colorado, http://fiske.colorado.edu/

Boulder: Henrietta Leavitt Flat Screen Space Theater, U. of Colorado, www.thespacewriter.com/

Denver: Gates Planetarium, www.dmns.org/main/en/General/Planetarium/CurrentShows/

#### Connecticut
Mystic: Planetarium, Mystic Seaport Museum,

www.mysticseaport.org/index.cfm?fuseaction=home.viewPage&page_id=38664F4E-91E2-8A79-7AEC31C8A921F20A

New Britain: Copernican Observatory and Planetarium, www.ccsu.edu/astronomy/

West Hartford: Gengras Planetarium, The Children's Museum,
www.thechildrensmuseumct.org/planetarium.htm

#### District of Columbia
Washington: Planetarium, Rock Creek Park Nat. Park Svc., Nat. Cap. Reg.
http://www.nps.gov/rocr/planetarium/

Washington: Albert Einstein Planetarium, National Air and Space Museum,
http://www.nasm.si.edu/NASMDOCS/PLANETARIUM/

## Florida

Bradenton: Bishop Planetarium, South Florida Museum,
http://southfloridamuseum.org/planetarium/default.html

Davie: Buehler Planetarium, Broward Community College, www.iloveplanets.com

Jacksonville: Alexander Brest Planetarium, Museum of Science and History (MOSH),
http://www.themosh.org/planetarium/index.asp

Miami: Miami Space Transit, Planetarium, www.miamisci.org/www/eventsplan.html

Orlando: John Young Planetarium, Orlando Science Center, www.osc.org/

Tampa: The Saunders Planetarium, Museum of Science & Industry, www.mosi.org/planetarium.html

West Palm Beach: Buzz Aldrin Planetarium, South Florida Science Museum, www.sfsm.org/

## Georgia

Atlanta: Jim Cherry Memorial Planetarium Fernbank Science Center,
http://fsc.fernbank.edu/Facilities/aboutplt.html

Decatur: Planetarium, Bradley Observatory, Agnes Scott College, http://bradley.agnesscott.edu/

## Hawaii

Honolulu: Kilolani Planetarium, Bernice P. Bishop Museum,
www.bishopmuseum.org/planetarium/planetarium.html

Kaneohe: Hokulani Imaginarium, Windward Community College,
http://aerospace.wcc.hawaii.edu/imaginarium.html

## Idaho

Pocatello: ISU Planetarium, Idaho State University, www.physics.isu.edu/astronomy-club/astronight.html

## Illinois

Chicago: The Adler Planetarium, www.adlerplanetarium.org/

Joliet: Herbert Trackman Planetarium Joliet Junior College, www.jjc.cc.il.us/Planetarium/

Kankakee: Strickler Planetarium, Olivet Nazarene University, 815-939-5267

Normal: Physics Department Planetarium Illinois State University, www.phy.ilstu.edu/~trw/planet.html

Peoria: Planetarium, Lakeview Museum/Arts & Science, www.lakeview-museum.org/surfers-sschafer/PlanetariumSchedule.html

Rock Island: John Deere Planetarium, Augustana College, http://helios.augustana.edu/~dr/astronomy.html

## Indiana

Indianapolis: Holcomb Observatory. & Planetarium Butler University, www.butler.edu/holcomb/

Indianapolis: SpaceQuest Planetarium, The Children's Museum, www.childrensmuseum.org/

## Iowa

Cherokee: Sanford Planetarium, http://mail.cherokee.k12.ia.us/~sanford/plan.htm

## Kansas

Hutchinson: Cosmosphere, www.cosmo.org/

## Kentucky

Bowling Green: Hardin Planetarium, Western Kentucky University, http://physics.wku.edu/planetarium.html

Louisville: Rauch Memorial Planetarium University of Louisville, www.louisville.edu/planetarium/

Richmond: Arnim D. Hummel Planetarium Eastern Kentucky University, www.planetarium.eku.edu/

**Louisiana**

Kenner: Planetarium, Freeport McMoRan Daily Living Science Center, http://nightskydesign.com/

**Maine**

Portland: Southworth Planetarium, University of Southern Maine, www.usm.maine.edu/~planet/

**Maryland**

Annapolis: Planetarium, U. S. Naval Academy, www.nadn.navy.mil/Museum/

Catonsville: Banneker Planetarium, Community College of Baltimore County, 410-455-4560

Baltimore: Davis Planetarium, Maryland Science Center, www.mdsci.org/

Bel Air: Southampton Planetarium, Harford County Public Schools, www.harcosci.org/

Lanham-Seabrook: Planetarium, Howard B. Owens Science Center,
www.pgcps.org/%7Ehbowens/planetarium.html

Prince Frederick: Arthur Storer Planetarium, Calvert County Public Schools,
www.calvertnet.k12.md.us/schools/planetarium/planetarium.html

Westminster: Planetarium, Bear Branch Nature Center, www.westminsterastro.org/bearbranch.htm

**Massachusetts**

Boston: Charles Hayden Planetarium Boston Museum of Science, www.mos.org/doc/1005

Worcester: Alden Planetarium, part of the Ecotarium, www.ecotarium.org/

**Michigan**

East Lansing: Abrams Planetarium, Michigan State University, www.pa.msu.edu/abrams/

Grand Rapids: Roger B. Chaffee Planetarium Grand Rapids Public Museum, www.grmuseum.com/

Grosse Pointe: The Grosse Pointe Planetarium North High School,
http://staff.gpschools.org/maciola/webpages/kids.htm

Lansing: Planetarium, Lansing Community College, www.sciencehobbies.com/planet.html

**Minnesota**

Duluth: Marshall Alworth Planetarium Univ. of Minnesota – Duluth, www.d.umn.edu/~planet/

Minneapolis: Minneapolis Planetarium, Friends of the Minneapolis Public Library,
www.mplanetarium.org/

**Mississippi**

Jackson: Ronald E. McNair Space Theater Russell C. Davis Planetarium,
www.city.jackson.ms.us/CityHall/planetarium.htm

**Missouri**

Kansas City: Planetarium, The Kansas City Museum, www.unionstation.org/planetarium.cfm

St. Louis: McDonnell Planetarium, St. Louis Science Center,
http://dev.golamacstaging.com/content.aspx?id=1899

**Montana**

Bozeman: Taylor Planetarium, Museum of the Rockies, www.montana.edu/wwwmor/index.html

**Nebraska**

Lincoln: Ralph Mueller Planetarium, University of Nebraska, http://www.spacelaser.com/

Omaha: Mallory Kountze Planetarium Univ. of Nebraska at Omaha, www.physics.unomaha.edu/planet/

**Nevada**

North Las Vegas: The Planetarium, Comm. Coll. of Southern Nevada,
www.ccsn.edu/about/campuslife/planetarium/index.aspx

Reno: Fleischmann Planetarium, University of Nevada, Reno, http://planetarium.unr.nevada.edu/

**New Jersey**

Newark: Dreyfuss Planetarium, Newark Museum, P.O. Box 540, www.newarkmuseum.org/planetarium/index.htm

Toms River: Robert J. Novins Planetarium Ocean County College, www.fieldtrip.com/nj/82550342.htm

**New Mexico**

Alamogordo: Clyde W. Tombaugh Space Theater Int'l. Space Hall of Fame, www.spacefame.org/

**New York**

Albany: Henry Hudson Planetarium,
www.albany.org/pages/visitorscenter/show_planetarium.asp?hd=Henry%20Hudson%20
Planetarium&sort=planetarium

Binghamton: Edwin A. Link Planetarium, Roberson Center, www.roberson.org/education/index.asp

Centerport, L.I.: Vanderbilt Planetarium, www.vanderbiltmuseum.org/home.php?section=planetarium

Fishkill: Gustafson Planetarium at Sharpe Reservation, http://www.sharpe.freshair.org/planetarium.htm

New Paltz: John R. Kirk Planetarium, S. U. College at New Paltz, www.newpaltz.edu/planetarium/

New York: American. Museum of Natural History. - Hayden Planetarium,
http://haydenplanetarium.org/index.phper

Rochester: Strasenburgh Planetarium, Rochester Museum & Science Center,
www.rmsc.org/planetarium/planetframeset.htm

Schenectady: Planetarium, Schenectady Museum, www,schenectadymuseum.org/

Syracuse: Planetarium, Milton J. Rubenstein Museum of Science & Technology,
http://www.most.org/2_index_interior_body.cfm

Yonkers: Andrus Planetarium, Hudson River Museum, www.hrm.org/planetarium.html

**North Carolina**

Chapel Hill: Morehead Planetarium, University of N. Carolina-C.H.,
http://moreheadplanetarium.org/index.cfm?fuseaction=page&filename=unc_science_news.html

**North Dakota**

Grand Forks: Center For Aerospace Sciences Atmospherium, Univ. of North Dakota,
www.und.edu/org/nsas/nsas.html

**Ohio**

Bowling Green: Planetarium, 104 Overman Hall Bowling Green State University,
http://physics.bgsu.edu/planetarium/

Cleveland: Shafran Planetarium, Cleveland Museum Nat. History, www.cmnh.org/

Delaware: Planetarium, Perkins Observatory, www.perkins-observatory.org/

Kent: Planetarium, Dept. of Physics Kent State University, http://planetarium.kent.edu/users/planet/

Toledo: Ritter Planetarium and Brooks Observatory, Univ. of Toledo, www.rpbo.utoledo.edu/

Youngstown: Ward Beecher Planetarium, Youngstown State University,
http://cc.ysu.edu/physics-astro/planet.htm

## Oklahoma

Oklahoma City: Kirkpatrick Planetarium, Omniplex Science & Arts Museum, http://www.omniplex.org/

Shawnee: W. B. Wood Planetarium, Oklahoma Baptist University,

## Oregon

Eugene: Lane E. S. D. Planetarium, Lane Education Service Dist.

Portland: Murdock Sky Theater, O. M. S. I., http://www.omsi.edu/

Salem: Chemeketa Community College Planetarium, (503) 399-5200,

Sunriver: The Sunriver Nature Center & Observatory, (541) 593-4394

## Pennsylvania

Allentown: Allentown S. Dist. Planetarium Louis E. Dieruff High School www.planetarium.org/

Harrisburg: Planetarium, State Museum of Pennsylvania, www.statemuseumpa.org/planet.html

Lancaster: Franklin and Marshall's North Museum, www.northmuseum.org/planetarium.htm

Philadelphia: Fels Planetarium, Franklin Institute Science Museum, http://sln.fi.edu/tfi/info/fels.html

Pittsburgh: Henry Buhl, Jr. Planetarium Carnegie Science Center, http://www.buhlplanetarium.org/

Reading: Reading Public Museum and Planetarium, http://planetarium.readingpublicmuseum.org/

Warminster: Henry W. Ray Special Experience Room, McDonald Elementary School,
     www.centennialsd.org/Community/SER/

## Rhode Island

Providence: Cormack Planetarium, Museum of Natural History, www.osfn.org/museum/

## South Carolina

Aiken: DuPont Planetarium, Ruth, Patrick Science Ed. Ctr., USC, http://rpsec.usca.sc.edu/dupontplanetarium/

Greenville: Howell Memorial Planetarium Bob Jones University, www.bju.edu/about/campus/science.html

Orangeburg: Stanback Planetarium, I. P. Stanback Museum, http://www.draco.scsu.edu/

Rock Hill: Settlemyre Planetarium, Museum of York County,
     www.chmuseums.org/ourmuseums/myco/planetarium.htm

## Tennessee

Jackson: M. D. Anderson Planetarium Lambuth University www.lambuth.edu/campuslife/planetarium.html,

Memphis: Sharpe Planetarium, Memphis Pink Palace Museum www.memphismuseums.org/planet.htm,

Nashville: Sudekum Planetarium, Cumberland Science Museum, www.sudekumplanetarium.com/

## Texas

Amarillo: Space Theater, Don Harrington Discovery Center www.dhdc.org/planetarium.html,

Fort Worth: Noble Planetarium, Museum of Science & History www.fwmuseum.org/noble/index.html,

Houston: Burke Baker Planetarium, Houston Museum of Natural Science, www.hmns.org/index.asp

Lubbock: Moody Planetarium, The Museum, Texas Tech University, http://interoz.com/lubbock/TTMUSEUM.htm

San Antonio: Scobee Planetarium, www.accd.edu/sac/ce/scobee/MainMenu.htm

## Utah

Provo: Sarah Summerhayes Planetarium Brigham Young University, http://planetarium.byu.edu/

Salt Lake City: Hansen Planetarium, www.hansenplanetarium.net/

## Vermont

St. Johnsbury: The Planetarium at, Fairbanks Museum & Planetarium, www.fairbanksmuseum.org/

**Virginia**

    Arlington: Arlington Planetarium, Arlington Public Schools www.arlington.k12.va.us/instruct/science/planetarium/,

    Newport News: Peninsula Planetarium, Virginia Living Museum, www.valivingmuseum.org/

    Richmond: Ethyl Universe Planetarium Science Museum of Virginia, http://www.smv.org/astro/index.html

    Roanoke: Hopkins Planetarium, Science Museum of Western Virginia, http://www.smwv.org/

**Washington**

    Bellingham: Planetarium, Physics/Astronomy Dept. Western Washington University,
        www.wwu.edu/depts/skywise/

    Seattle: Willard W. Smith Planetarium Pacific Science Center, www.pacsci.org/planetarium/

**Wisconsin**

    Madison: Madison Metro S.D. Planetarium James Madison Memorial High School,
        www.madison.k12.wi.us/planetarium/

**Wyoming**

    Casper: Casper Planetarium, Natrona County School District,
        http://ncsdweb.ncsd.k12.wy.us/planetarium/history.htm

## Where to Catch the Best Sunrises & Sunsets in the United States

Anchorage, Alaska: Watch the Sun descend over snow-capped mountains

Arizona: Who can argue that the sunset over the Grand Canyon isn't amazing?

California: View the sunset in San Francisco Bay behind the Golden Gate Bridge

California: Get up early and watch the sunrise over Half Dome in Yosemite National Park

Florida: Watch for the green flash right before the Sun sets on Captiva Island

Hawaii: Catch the sunrise at Haleakala National Park on Maui

Massachusetts: Catch a Cape Cod sunrise

## The Dark-Sky Calendar

January: Look for Saturn at the end of the month in the dark sky

February: A good time to look for Venus, Mars, Jupiter and Saturn

March: Enjoy the full moon the Dakotah Sioux call "Moon When Eyes Are Sore from Bright Snow"

April: National Dark-Sky Week (week of the new moon): www.ndsw.org/

May: National Astronomy Day (a Saturday near the first quarter moon):
    www.astroleague.org/al/astroday/astrofacts.html

June: Summer solstice on June 21

July: Find Jupiter in the night sky

August: Perseid Meteor Showers

September: Autumnal Equinox

October: Look for Mars

November: Leonid Meteor Showers

December: Gemini Meteor Showers

# Index